CULTURES OF THE WORLD

Myanmar

Marshall Cavendish Benchmark
New York

PICTURE CREDITS
Cover: © Hemis.fr/SuperStock
Anders Blomqvist/Lonely Planet Images: 96 • Antony Giblin/Lonely Planet Images: 84 • Austin Bush/Lonely Planet Images: 106 • Bernard Napthine/Lonely Planet Images: 5, 51, 54, 56, 103, 117 • Christian Holst/Edit by Getty Images: 29 • Christopher Groenhout/Lonely Planet Images: 126 • CKN/Getty Images: 32 • Danita Delimont /Getty Images: 105 • Father Browne/Universal Images Group/Getty Images: 26 • Felix Hug/Lonely Planet Images: 85, 93, 102, 116 • Frank Carter/Lonely Planet Images: 50, 125 • Inmagine: 3, 6, 7, 8, 9, 20, 34, 35, 36, 40, 42, 58, 59, 70, 73, 77, 80, 86, 94, 104, 110 • Jane Sweeney/Lonely Planet Images: 75 • Johnny Haglund/ Lonely Planet Images: 53 • Manfred Gottschalk/Lonely Planet Images: 88 • Patrick Aventurier/Gamma-Rapho via Getty Images: 107 • Paul Chesley/Getty Images: 115 • Pete Turner/Getty Images: 47 • Photolibrary: 10, 11, 12, 16, 23, 39, 44, 45, 52, 60, 61, 62, 64, 65, 67, 68, 72, 76, 92, 97, 100, 113, 118, 120, 121, 128, 130 • Picture Post/ Hulton Archive/Getty Images: 25 • Rachel Lewis/Lonely Planet Images: 1, 74, 78, 123 • Richard I'Anson/Lonely Planet Images: 122 • Sandro Tucci//Time Life Pictures/Getty Images: 30 • Soe Than Win/AFP/Getty Images: 28, 31 • Steve Winter/Getty Images: 48 • Tim Hill / Alamy: 131 • Zaw Min Yu/Lonely Planet Images: 15, 111

PRECEDING PAGE
A young girl with her brother wearing *thanaka* (traditional sunscreen) on their cheeks.

Publisher (U.S.): Michelle Bisson
Writers: Saw Myat Yin and Josie Elias
Editors: Deborah Grahame-Smith, Stephanie Pee
Copyreader: Tara Tomczyk
Designers: Nancy Sabato, Lock Hong Liang, Steven Tan
Cover picture researcher: Tracey Engel
Picture researcher: Joshua Ang

Marshall Cavendish Benchmark
99 White Plains Road
Tarrytown, NY 10591
Website: www.marshallcavendish.us

Originated and designed by Times Media Private Limited
An imprint of Marshall Cavendish International (Asia) Private Limited
A member of Times Publishing Limited

Library of Congress Cataloging-in-Publication Data
Yin, Saw Myat, 1946-
Myanmar / Saw Myat Yin & Josie Elias. — 3rd ed.
p. cm. — (Cultures of the world)
Summary: "Provides comprehensive information on the geography, history, wildlife, governmental structure, economy, cultural diversity, peoples, religion, and culture of Myanmar"—Provided by publisher.
Includes bibliographical references and index.
ISBN 978-1-60870-786-7 (print)
1. Burma—Juvenile literature. I. Elias, Josie. II. Title. III. Series.

DS527.4.Y564 2012
959.1—dc22 2011004478

Printed in Malaysia
7 6 5 4 3 2 1

CONTENTS

MYANMAR TODAY

MYANMAR, OR THE REPUBLIC OF THE UNION OF MYANMAR, as it is now officially named, is a country little known to the rest of the world, even to its Asian neighbors. For more than a quarter of a century, it has been so isolated that it seems to have almost disappeared from the map of the world. One of Southeast Asia's largest and most diverse countries, it stretches from the sparkling coral islands of the Andaman Sea in the south right up into the snow-covered Eastern Himalayan mountain range. Myanmar is often known as the land of pagodas. Yet there is more to Myanmar than that. It has virgin jungles, pristine beaches, and snow-capped mountains, combined with a rich heritage spanning more than 2,000 years. Monuments and ancient cities provide evidence of a lively culture that is home to more than 135 ethnic groups. Its cultural life is a rich and unique mix of Buddhist teachings and elements of Hindu culture. The Myanmar, regardless of whether they are country folk or urbanites, are a warm and friendly people who always have time to sit and exchange tales or the latest jokes over a cup of tea.

The ramparts of the Mandalay royal palace.

For the last 36 years Myanmar has been ruled by a military government, the *tatmadaw*, led by Senior General Than Shwe, who assumed office after the elections in 1992 despite a reputed landslide victory for the National League for Democracy (NLD). The junta refused to cede power, and placed the NLD leader Aung San Suu Kyi under house arrest.

It has still been possible to travel to Myanmar, but the number of visitors has dropped dramatically because the country has been deemed off-limits to foreign visitors for the last 15 years. For all its absence from mainstream travel itineraries, the celebrated names on the nation's map still conjure up some of the most exotic and exciting destinations in the Far East: the former capital and fabled royal city of Mandalay and Bagan, a 13th-century

Pagodas and stupas dot the landscape of Myanmar, a testament to its Buddhist faith.

extravaganza of dazzling golden Buddhist temples and stupas that led Marco Polo to dub Myanmar the "Golden Land."

Myanmar is a resource-rich country and it was one of the more developed countries in Asia but it has suffered under extensive government controls and inefficient economic policies that caused widespread rural poverty. Myanmar has many unique attractions: literally thousands of pagodas, a fascinating culture, and rich and varied landscapes. However, the unstable political situation discourages many potential tourists from visiting, and certain areas in Myanmar are out of bounds because of recent political disturbances. A general election was held on November 7, 2010, and amidst international cries of election fraud and other irregularities, the Union Solidarity and Development Party were eventually declared the victors.

GEOGRAPHY

The valley of the Mula in the Phon Kan Razi Wildlife Sanctuary is part of Myanmar's beautiful and varied terrain.

1

MYANMAR IS A LAND of contrasts in landscapes, with snowy mountains in the far north and sunny, tropical beaches in the south.

GEOGRAPHICAL LOCATION

Myanmar lies in mainland Southeast Asia, bordered by India in the northwest, Bangladesh and the Bay of Bengal in the west, the Andaman Sea in the south, China in the north and northeast, and Laos and Thailand in the east.

Apart from a 1,199-mile-long (1,930-kilometer-long) coastline, Myanmar is surrounded by a horseshoe-shaped ring of mountains

A river meanders quietly through the Myo Gyi Shan State.

Myanmar lies in Southeast Asia and has a land mass slightly smaller than the state of Texas. It boasts a strategic location near major Indian Ocean shipping lanes. The country is rich in natural resources but lies within an area of destructive earthquakes and cyclones, with flooding and landslides common during the rainy season.

Myanmar is prone to heavy monsoon rains.

that form a natural border of 3,651 miles (5,876 km) with its neighbors. The main rivers are the Ayeyarwady, Chindwin, Thanlwin, and Sittaung. The country covers 261,228 square miles (676,578 square km) and consists of the seven states of Rakhine, Chin, Kachin, Kayin (or Karen), Kayah, Shan, and Mon.

SEASONS

Myanmar experiences three seasons in a year: the rainy season (monsoon) from July to October, a cold season from November to February, and a hot season from March to June. Rainfall is as much as 200 inches (508 centimeters) a year in the coastal regions, 100 inches (254 cm) in the plains, and averages under 40 inches (101.6 cm) in the central part. Temperatures reach 113°F (45°C) in central Myanmar, and fall to 32°F (0°C) in the north. The average annual temperature varies from 71°F (22°C) in the highlands of the Shan plateau to 81°F (27°C) in the southern lowlands.

Myanmar can be roughly divided into four regions: the northern and western mountainous region, the eastern Shan plateau, the central belt, and the long southern "tail." The region north of Mandalay is commonly referred to as Upper Myanmar, while Yangon and the Ayeyarwady delta are known as Lower Myanmar.

NORTHERN AND WESTERN REGIONS

The northern and western mountains extend from the extreme north down to the western side of Myanmar. The Kachin, Chin, and Rakhine states are located in this region. Some of Myanmar's highest peaks are here: Mount Hkakabo Razi (19,296 feet/5,881 meters), which is the highest in Southeast Asia; Mount Gamlan Razi, which, along with Mount Hkakabo, is in the extreme northern part of the Kachin range; and Mount Sarameti and Mount Victoria in the Chin range.

Rakhine State in the west has a coastal strip that is wide in the north and narrows toward the south. The resort beaches are located here. Offshore numerous islands dot the Bay of Bengal and the Andaman Sea.

The vegetation in this region varies from tropical and subtropical to temperate and alpine forests. There is an abundance of rhododendron, magnolia, juniper, pine, birch, and cherry trees here. Bamboo forests cover a large area of the Rakhine range. Wild animals still survive in the mountains—bears, civet cats, elephants, leopards, and tigers, to name a few. The rare takin (*Budorcas taxicolor*), red panda (*Ailurus fulgens*), Malayan tapir (*Tapirus indicus*), snow leopard (*Panthera uncia*), and Siberian musk

Ngapali Beach, part of the Rakhine coast.

The Malayan tapir is a rare sight in Myanmar now, due to a combination of destruction of its habitat and hunting.

deer (*Moschus moschiferus*) are found in the northern temperate forests, although some of these animals have been hunted to near extinction.

The capitals of the states of Kachin, Chin, and Rakhine are Myitkyina, Falam, and Sittwe, respectively. In Kachin State the confluence of the Nmai Hka and Mali rivers gives rise to the Ayeyarwady River, which is the country's largest river and most important waterway.

CENTRAL REGION

The central region has a dry zone, but here are also the rich river valleys and plains of the mighty Ayeyarwady, the Chindwin—a tributary of the Ayeyarwady—and the Sittaung rivers. Low mountain ranges flank many of the river valleys.

In the dry zone the flora consists of thorny trees and shrubs and cacti. Snakes, especially poisonous vipers, are particularly common here. Petroleum and gas are found in the central region, and agricultural products such as beans, pulses, cotton, onions, chili, oilseeds, and tobacco are also produced here.

Teak and other hardwoods cover the slopes of the mountain ranges, while in the river valleys and plains, the main crop is rice. Jute and sugarcane, important industrial raw materials, are also grown here. Fish and shrimp are bred in ponds and harvested from rivers and creeks.

The main cities in this area are: Yangon (or Rangoon), the capital; Pathein; and Bago, the ancient Mon capital, which is 47 miles (76 km) northeast of Yangon. Pyi and Toungoo are also historical capitals. Ancient

MYANMAR'S LIFELINE

The Ayeyarwady River is Myanmar's lifeline. It is 1,350 miles (2,172 km) long. Its source is in the Himalayas, and it flows down the middle of Myanmar to the Andaman Sea. It divides Myanmar; most of the towns are on the east bank. The country's historical capitals, such as Mandalay, Innwa, Amarapura, Pye (or Pyay), and Pagan (Bagan), are also on this side. Only one bridge, the Innwa bridge near Mandalay, spanned the Ayeyarwady until the 1990s. All other crossings are made by boats of all sizes and shapes, from large car ferries to narrow, long rowboats.

The Ayeyarwady is the backbone of the country's transportation system. On this great river one can see steamers carrying passengers and cargo, barges on which families spend their entire lives carrying products up and down the river, and great rafts of bamboo or teak floating down to Yangon for export.

pagodas and ruins of older habitation can still be seen in these cities today. Other important cities in the dry central region are Mandalay, Monywa, Magway, and Pakokku.

AYEYARWADY DELTA

The delta in the south, where the river divides into eight main branches before flowing into the Andaman Sea, is Myanmar's "rice bowl." It is estimated that 60 to 70 percent of rice production comes from this area, and it is famous for fish and shrimp and products derived from them. The delta covers 19,500 square miles (50,400 square km) and is a veritable network of streams and creeks. The area is fertile and rich in alluvial soil as low as just 9.8 feet (3 m) above sea level.

The delta region is densely populated. On May 2, 2008, the area was devastated by Cyclone Nargis, which reportedly killed more than 84,500 people, with 53,800 missing, and rendered about 2.4 million homeless, mostly in the southwest delta region.

SHAN PLATEAU

The Shan plateau in eastern Myanmar is a tableland about 3,000 feet (914 m) above sea level that forms the border with China, Laos, and Thailand. The Thanlwin River, Myanmar's longest at 1,750 miles (2,816 km), rises in Tibet and flows down the plateau through narrow gorges. The Shan State is in the northern part of the plateau, and Kayah State is in the southern part. The climate on the plateau is cool all year-round.

Pine and cherry trees grow wild here, as do many wild orchids found on trees and rocky clefts; the blue vanda orchid (*Vanda coerulea*) is a native of the Shan plateau.

Tea; fruits such as avocados, pears, oranges, tangerines, and strawberries; and vegetables such as carrots, cabbages, kohlrabi, beans, and peas are cultivated here. Opium poppies (*Papaver somniferum*) are grown in the part of the Shan State that is included in the Golden Triangle, one of Asia's two main illicit opium-producing areas that overlap the mountains of Myanmar, Vietnam, Laos, and Thailand. The majority of the people who live in this part of the Shan State have been fighting a protracted war with the central government for autonomy.

Mogok, in western Shan State, is famous for its rubies, sapphires, and other gems. Lead, silver, tin, tungsten, and marble are also obtained from this area.

TANINTHARYI COASTAL STRIP

The Tanintharyi coastal strip that includes the states of Mon and Tanintharyi is the long "tail" of Myanmar that extends from the Shan plateau down to the isthmus of Kra in the south. The mountain ranges in the east form a natural border with Thailand. Tin and tungsten are mined in this region, and forests are logged.

The only available agricultural land here is a narrow strip between the mountains and the sea. The land is well used, with rice being the main crop. Orchards grow tropical fruits such as pineapple, durian, rambutan, and mangosteen; roots such as tapioca; and nuts such as betel nut, cashew nut, and coconut. Rubber is also grown here.

Offshore fishing and related industries such as canning and preserving are found in the towns of Dawei and Myeik. The Tanintharyi coast has a number of resort beaches, but these are inaccessible to foreigners because the area is considered unsafe due to security concerns from the general threat of terrorism, mugging, burglaries and petty theft.

The crowded and confusing streets of Chinatown in Yangon.

The capitals of Mon State and Tanintharyi—Mawlamyine and Dawei, respectively—are trading centers for goods from neighboring Thailand.

MYEIK ARCHIPELAGO

The Myeik archipelago is a group of about 800 islands off the Tanintharyi coast opposite the town of Myeik. The Salon people who live here are known as sea gypsies and are famous for deep-sea diving for pearls and abalone. They live on boats near the islands but move to the land in the rainy season. They were once feared as pirates of the Andaman Sea.

TRANSPORTATION

Myanmar's roads and railways follow the north-to-south physical arrangement of rivers and mountain ranges. The few east-to-west roads cross mountain ranges. Many rivers also impede road travel.

The roads and railways are a heritage from British colonizers, and further development has been slow due to economic stagnation and the political isolation, which has barred international aid.

Yangon is a densely populated city. It was once the capital of Myanmar and remains its largest city to this day.

Rivers and inland waterways are important for trade and transportation, especially the Ayeyarwady and Sittaung rivers and their tributaries in the delta. River crafts are mostly crowded, old private steamers. The northern portion of the Sittaung and Thanlwin rivers is not navigable, but these rivers are useful as chutes for floating down teak, other hardwoods, and bamboo that have been extracted from the forests.

Myanmar's original and only national airline was renamed Myanma Airways in 1988 when Burma was officially renamed Myanmar. In 1993 a new airline, Myanmar Airways International (MAI), was incorporated as a joint venture between Myanma Airways and Singapore interests with the support of Royal Brunei Airlines. MAI's potential continued to attract investors and in February 2007, a new joint venture was formed in which Myanma Airways retained 51 percent and Region Air (HK) Ltd., took a 49 percent stake.

CITIES

Many place names in Myanmar were Anglicized by the British when they occupied the country in the 19th century. The present government has restored the Myanmar names to most of the towns and cities.

NAYPYIDAW, or Abode of Kings, was officially proclaimed the capital of the country in 2007. It is a new city, built on a vast and extravagant scale in an area of tropical scrubland, about 300 miles (460 km) north of the old capital, Rangoon. Ministry buildings and apartments are being built for all government employees, and the military has a complex to the east of the

THE SHWE DAGON

The Shwe Dagon, on Singuttara Hill in Yangon, is Myanmar's most sacred pagoda. It enshrines the Buddha's hair and other holy relics. Originally only 27 feet (8 m) high, it is now 326 feet (99 m) in height after successive renovations and additions that were made by kings and queens.

Gold and precious gems adorn the pagoda and are also buried in the main treasure chamber under the spire. Four staircases (each with about 130 steps) lead to the pagoda, which is surrounded by numerous smaller spires and monasteries. The main platform and surrounding terraces are always full of worshipers who are meditating or praying, and offering flowers, food, candles, and water.

city. This is where Myanmar's leader, General Than Shwe, now lives. Much of the city is still under construction, due for completion around 2012.

YANGON RANGOON, renamed its Burmese name Yangon in 1989, was Myanmar's capital from 1948 to 2007 when the new city of Naypyidaw became the capital of the country. Founded in 1755 by King Alaungpaya, Yangon grew into a trading port after the British annexed lower Burma in 1826. It became the capital after all of Burma fell to the British in 1886, only to be stripped of this title in 2007.

Yangon, which is accessible to foreigners only by sea or air, is a vibrant and dynamic city and a hub of economic activity. The superb Shwedagon Pagoda is visible from all over town with its gleaming golden stupa. Closer to the waterfront downtown, Yangon conceals some of the best British colonial architecture in its warren of historic streets. The population was more than 4 million in 2007, with ethnic Myanmar being the majority.

MANDALAY Mandalay is Myanmar's second-largest city and main cultural center, with a population of 960,000 in 2007. It lies on the eastern bank of the Ayeyarwady, about 500 miles (805 km) north of Yangon. Established in 1857 by King Mindon, it was Myanmar's last capital before the country

BAGAN

Bagan is situated on the east bank of the Ayeyarwady, about 120 miles (193 km) south of Mandalay. Its 16 square miles (41 square km) are covered by countless pagodas and temples, which date from the 11th century onward; some are in ruins and some stand in gilded splendor.

Bagan was first established as a walled city in A.D. 874. Beginning with King Anawrahta's reign in 1044, Bagan became a powerful kingdom stretching to Bamaw in the north; Thanlwin in the east; Assam, Rakhine, and the Chin hills in the west; and the Mon kingdom in the south. Anawrahta conquered the Mon people in 1057 and brought to Bagan the king and royal family, artisans, craftspeople, and Theravada Buddhism, which flourished under successive kings who built many pagodas. The architecture, frescoes, murals, plaster carvings, and bas-reliefs of these pagodas have been described as marvelous relics of Bagan's glory. Bagan fell to the Mongols in 1287, and most of the temples are said to have been pulled down by the Myanmar in an attempt to fortify themselves. Bagan's dry climate, probably resulting from excessive felling of trees for firewood to feed brick kilns where pagoda bricks were made, has helped preserve these precious monuments, which have remained as places of worship.

Many pagodas were destroyed by an earthquake in 1975, but international agencies have helped with restoration work. The villagers who once lived in Bagan have been relocated, and the entire area has been closed to settlements.

came under British rule. The magnificent Mandalay palace was burned down during World War II. A replica was rebuilt in the 1990s on the palace grounds, which are surrounded by a moat. Many ancient pagodas and monasteries still stand in Mandalay.

Mandalay is famous not only for being a center of Buddhist learning and fine arts, but also for its gold and silver crafts, carving, and weaving. It is a trading center for agricultural and other products from all parts of Upper Myanmar.

MAWLAMYINE Formerly Moulmein, Mawlamyine is the third-largest city and is situated at the mouth of the Thanlwin River. It is an important port and trading center for both products of the Tanintharyi area and those that arrive overland from neighboring countries. The Thanlwin bridge, stretching over a distance of 11,000 feet (3,352 m), is the longest road bridge in Myanmar and is a prominent landmark connecting the southeastern region with Yangon. Mawlamyine is famous for its fruit, and the women of the area usually possess great culinary skill.

PATHEIN Pathein, or Bassein, is Myanmar's second-largest port city with a 2004 population estimate of 215,600. It is 28 miles (45 km) from the sea on the Pathein River and is the capital of the Ayeyarwady Region. The city is a rice-milling and export center and is also famous for fish, shrimp, their derived products, and colorful hand-painted umbrellas.

INTERNET LINKS

www.ancientbagan.com/index.htm

A website devoted to the history and monuments to be found in Bagan. It includes sections on lifestyle, festivals, and events as well as information for the visitor such as what festivals, shows, and events are on, how to get there, and where to stay.

www.ruby-sapphire.com/pigeons-blood-mogok.htm

Information on the ruby-mining techniques employed in Mogok is found in an article entitled "Pigeon's Blood—A Pilgrimage to Mogok—Valley of Rubies," by Richard W. Hughes.

www.tapirs.org/tapirs/malay.html

Tapir Specialist Group is a global group of biologists, zoo professionals, researchers, and advocates dedicated to conserving tapirs and their habitat, and to emphasizing the importance of the tapir to local ecosystems and to the world at large.

HISTORY

The ancient city of Bagan.

2

THE AYEYARWADY VALLEY WAS inhabited some 5,000 years ago by Neolithic man, hunters and gatherers who used stone and wood tools. Farther north, in the eastern part of the Shan State, cave paintings and stone tools show that there were other early settlers here as well. The Anyathians and the Shan cave people stayed far from the sea. The earliest settlers on the coast were the Negritos who came from Indonesia.

Myanmar has a long and complex history with many varied peoples inhabiting the region through time. Humans have lived in Myanmar for at least 15,000 years. Marco Polo was the first Westerner to arrive in Myanmar in 1287. He described the glittering golden pagodas in his writings, dubbing the country "The Golden Land."

ARRIVAL OF THE FIRST BAMARS

A few centuries before Christ, the Mons entered Myanmar from the region that is now Thailand and Cambodia, and settled around the mouths of the Thanlwin and Sittaung rivers. They cultivated and exported rice as well as teak, minerals, and ivory to India, Arabia, China, and Indochina.

At about the same time, some Tibeto-Myanmar tribes, including the Pyus and their allied tribes, left their homeland on the southeastern slopes of the Tibetan plateau and migrated south, entering the upper Ayeyarwady valley. The Pyus, a loosely knit group of tribes who disappeared in the eighth century, were the first migrants to found a great kingdom, at Pyi. The Pyus were a graceful people, who were devout

Theravada Buddhists. Some centuries later the Pyus were pushed back by the Mons. In the process the Bamars (known as Burmans, anthropologically), a people who had been subject to the Pyus, rose to prominence.

In the 12th century the Shans, also known as Tai, arrived from Yunnan, northeast of Myanmar. The Bamars of today are descendants of the Mons, the Bamars, the Pyus, and the Shans.

FIRST BAMAR EMPIRE (1044–1287)

After the Pyus were pushed north by the Mons, the Bamars established a small settlement of their own and founded the city of Bagan in A.D. 847. After many dynastic struggles during the first two centuries of Bagan's existence, Anawrahta, a Bamar military leader, became king of Bagan in A.D. 1044. During his reign of 33 years, he conquered the Mons, brought Buddhism to Bagan, and united all parts of modern Myanmar except for the Shan plateau and parts of Rakhine and Tanintharyi. His reign was known as the First Myanmar Empire and marked the beginning of Myanmar as a distinct political entity. The kingdom survived until 1287, when it fell to the armies of Kublai Khan. For the next three centuries disunity characterized Myanmar, which disintegrated into small states.

Taking advantage of the turmoil ensuing the fall of the First Bamar Empire, the Mons moved south and founded a new kingdom in Bago in Lower Myanmar. The Shans also broke away and extended their territory westward, establishing a capital in Innwa on the banks of the Ayeyarwady. The remaining Bamars withdrew to Toungoo on the Sittaung River to await an opportunity to initiate the reunification of Myanmar, which did not happen for another 260 years.

SECOND BAMAR EMPIRE (1551–1752)

In 1541 the Bamars under King Tabinshwehti (1531—50) took advantage of the frequent wars between the Shans and Mons and captured Innwa and Bago. After Tabinshwehti's death, however, the kingdom again fell apart.

King Tabinshwehti's brother-in-law and successor, King Bayinnaung (1551—81), later reconquered all the lost territory, won Chiang Mai and Ayuthia from the Siamese, and took back Tanintharyi, thus founding the Second Bamar Empire. Other states on the Myanmar-Chinese border and Manipur, now part of India, paid tribute to Myanmar.

An illustration of the King's Pagoda in Mandalay, dated around 1885.

During this period trade with neighboring countries developed; Bago became an important port for traders traveling to China via the Ayeyarwady and northern Myanmar. It was also a convenient stop for traders going to other parts of Southeast Asia by way of Thanlyin, Mottama, and Pathein, which were important ports in Lower Burma.

Foreigners, especially Arabs and Portuguese, were very active in east-west trade. The British, French, and Dutch trading companies were established in Burma in the 17th century when the capital was moved from Bago to Innwa. During the 18th century the Shans became weaker, and the Mons, with help from the French, captured Innwa in 1752.

THIRD BAMAR EMPIRE (1752—1885)

After conquering Innwa, the Mons tried to control all of Myanmar until the Bamar headman of a tiny Shwebo village, Alaungpaya, defeated them. After eight years of war King Alaungpaya was able to unite the country again and founded the Konbaung dynasty, the third and last Bamar empire. He also moved the capital to Innwa.

Hsinbyushin, Alaungpaya's son and successor, invaded Siam (present-day Thailand) and destroyed Ayuthia in 1767. As a result Tanintharyi was again under Myanmar control. This victory brought to Myanmar Siamese dancers, musicians, and artisans who influenced Myanmar art and literature.

Another development during this time was the conquest of Rakhine by Hsinbyushin's brother, Bodawpaya. During his reign Bodawpaya (1782—1819) improved the tax collection, communications, legal, and educational systems.

During this dynasty, with few exceptions, the death of a king was followed by assassinations and rebellions. The lack of a system for appointing a successor to the throne was one of the reasons for the disunity among the Bamars, which resulted in the eventual fall of the Third Bamar Empire.

BRITISH RULE (1886—1942)

In 1886, after three wars with the British, Burma became a British colony. The three Anglo-Myanmar wars in 1824—1826, 1852, and 1885 had their origin in British economic and political interests in Burma.

After the first war Burma lost Rakhine and Tanintharyi. In 1852 the British annexed Lower Burma in order to close the gap between Calcutta and Singapore, and they made it a province of British India. In 1885 Burma tried to make contact with the outside world, especially France, during the reign of the last king, Thibaw (1881—85). The British, who feared French interference and wanted a monopoly in teak, used a dispute between Burma and a British timber firm, accused of illegal logging, as an excuse to march to Mandalay, the capital at that time. In 1886 all of Burma became a province of British India, and the Burmese royal family was exiled to India.

The British introduced the classic divide-and-rule principle, giving the minority states permission to be ruled by their own leaders. They did not recruit ethnic Myanmar for their army. All important posts in the civil service were filled by Indians or other foreigners. Burma's natural resources were exploited by foreigners and profits channeled out of the country. The British allowed Indians to migrate to Burma to alleviate labor shortages in the rice fields. All these factors inspired the Myanmar nationalists to rebel against the British.

In the early 20th century the nationalist movement, under the leadership of the Young Men's Buddhist Association (YMBA) and Rangoon University

GENERAL AUNG SAN

General Aung San is Burma's national hero and the father of Burma's independence. He started his political career as a young student leader at Rangoon University, founding the Thakin movement together with other students. The members of this movement, dissatisfied with having to address the British as thakin *(master), and feeling that this demeaned the Myanmar people, termed themselves thakin and wore traditional Myanmar clothes.*

During World War II, General Aung San formed the Thirty Comrades, a group of 30 young men who swore a blood oath. They secretly went to Japan to ask for help and training to remove the British from Burma. The Japanese, however, proved to be ruthless when they came to Burma. Toward the end of World War II, Aung San and his Myanmar Independence Army sought the help of the British to drive out the Japanese.

After the war General Aung San continued to negotiate for independence, which was won on January 4, 1948. Sadly he did not live to see the day. On July 19, 1947, General Aung San was assassinated, together with six cabinet ministers, at the age of 32.

student leaders, grew in strength. During World War II, General Aung San initially collaborated with the Japanese, who made him promises of independence provided he would help them oust the British. In 1941 San and the Japanese did exactly that and the British retreated, losing thousands of men. After four years of fighting the allies were able to take Myanmar back. Aung San realized that the Japanese had their own imperialistic interests in Myanmar, and eventually sided with the allies. After the war the British finally gave Burma its independence.

Saopha Sao Shwe Thaik, a Shan chief and first independent president of Myanmar, inspects the country's troops.

AFTER INDEPENDENCE

U Nu became the first prime minister of independent Burma in 1948. After independence the country remained unsettled, with rebellions from the minorities who demanded their own autonomous states and the communists who had chosen to go underground. Indeed these insurrections continue to the present day—more than 60 years after independence.

Elections that should have been held soon after independence in 1948 were held three years later, after the army had managed to contain the rioting and regain control of the country. In the 1951 election the Anti-Fascist People's Freedom League (AFPFL) won. This political party was an offshoot of the Anti-Fascist Organization, a secret party formed during the Japanese occupation.

The political unrest continued to plague the new government. Economic development plans were implemented without much success. Export earnings fell because of to the decline of rice exports, and domestic revenue collection was hampered.

In the late 1950s, with the economy floundering, the AFPFL split into two groups—the "Clean" and the "Stable." As a result of armed clashes in the villages, a caretaker government, consisting of members of the armed forces, was asked to take over in 1958. During the two years of this government, the economy improved and government departments became more efficient.

Elections were held in 1960 to return the country to civil rule. The "Clean" AFPFL, renamed the Pyidaungsu Party, won. The insurrection problem, however, became more severe since the Shans favored secession.

On March 2, 1962, the army once more stepped in and took over the government in a coup d'état. Known as the Revolutionary Government, its highest body was the Revolutionary Council, composed of 17 high-ranking members of the armed forces. The government declared its socialist aims and abolished democracy. The country embarked on a policy of withdrawal and isolation, a self-sufficient economy, and strict neutrality in world politics.

Soon after the revolutionary government came to power, widespread nationalization of trading organizations, banks, industries, schools, and hospitals took place. Many foreigners were obliged to leave.

In 1974 a new constitution was adopted after a national referendum. The country became known as the Socialist Republic of the Union of Burma, and the Burma Socialist Programme Party (BSPP) was the only political party allowed.

In 1988 student-led demonstrations were suppressed by the military, which seized power in a coup d'état. The new government, formed by the State Law and Order Restoration Council (SLORC), initially changed the official name of the country to the Union of Burma, and in 1989 to the Union of Myanmar. It declared that the country was no longer on the socialist path. Efforts were made by the SLORC to actively seek foreign investments to modernize industries and build infrastructure projects. In addition the economy was opened to private entrepreneurs in the 1990s.

INTERNET LINKS

www.timetoast.com/timelines/9491

This site provides an interactive illustrated timeline about the history of Myanmar from A.D. 200 to 2000.

www.geographia.com/myanmar/

This website is an introduction to Myanmar, including information on the history and culture.

www.abitsu.org

The website of the All Burma I.T. Students' Union (ABITSU) includes a detailed section on the life of General Aung San.

GOVERNMENT

A Myanmar official prepares a polling station before elections.

3

MYANMAR IS AT PRESENT ruled by a military government that came to power after a coup d'état on September 18, 1988.

Prior to 1988 the country had a one-party socialist government. The Burma Socialist Programme Party (BSPP) had based its policies on "The Myanmar Way to Socialism," a program of socialism and Buddhism, declared on April 30, 1962. In 1974 a new constitution was adopted and a new flag and state seal were introduced. In October 2010 Myanmar's ruling military changed the flag, the state seal, the national anthem, and the official name of the country from the Union of Myanmar to the Republic of the Union of Myanmar.

Supporters of the National Democratic Front campaigning in Yangon.

Myanmar was a monarchy ruled by various dynasties before the British colonized it in the late 19th century. Until 1937, it was under the jurisdiction of the British Raj, the British government in India. Myanmar was ruled as a British colony from the 1820s until 1948, when the country achieved independence and became a parliamentary democracy.

The government consisted of the parliament (*Pyithu Hluttaw* or People's Assembly), made up of the Council of State and four subordinate organs of state power: the Council of Ministers, the Council of People's Justices, the Council of People's Attorneys, and the Council of People's Inspectors. The Council of State was elected by the parliament; the chairman of the Council of State was also the president of the Socialist Republic of the Union of Burma.

POLITICAL UPHEAVAL

A series of political events throughout 1988 caused an upheaval in the country's government. The chief reason for political unrest was poverty caused by years of economic mismanagement, a prolonged insurgency problem, and a heavy foreign debt. Beginning with student demonstrations, originating from a tea-shop brawl in the capital in early 1987, the revolt spread to include the general population in Rangoon, Mandalay, and other cities. The demonstrations became anarchic and violent throughout the

The usually reserved monks took to the streets to demonstrate against the then-government's policies. This political unrest eventually ended in tragedy and bloodshed.

months of July, August, and September 1988. The unrest was brutally suppressed, and finally resulted in a coup d'état on September 18, 1988. Martial law was imposed immediately after the coup and was not lifted until mid-1991.

The State Law and Order Restoration Council (SLORC), with local governing bodies called State Law and Order Restoration Committees at the state, division, township, sector, and ward levels, changed its name to the State Peace and Development Council (SPDC) in 1997.

National League for Democracy's charismatic leader, Aung San Suu Kyi, who was under house arrest for most of the last 20 years.

THE UNION OF MYANMAR

Soon after the coup the country was renamed the Union of Burma, which was later changed to the Union of Myanmar. Names of certain towns were also changed to their equivalents in the Myanmar language. Rangoon, the capital, was renamed Yangon.

The military government held the promised elections in May 1990. These were the first elections held since 1960. A large number of political parties (more than 200) registered with the General Elections Commission. The largest party, the National League for Democracy (NLD), won 392 seats and was headed by Daw Aung San Suu Kyi, the daughter of General Aung San. Although she was placed under house arrest in 1989, the NLD won the elections in a landslide victory. However, the SPDC never handed over power to NLD, and although Aung San Suu Kyi was awarded the Nobel Peace Prize in 1991, she remained under house arrest until 1995, after which her movements were still restricted. In 2000 she was detained again. She was sidelined for Burma's first elections in two decades on November 7, 2010, but was released from house arrest six days later.

A national convention, made up of various people from the councils of state power, has been drawing up a new constitution in which the military is expected to be given a major role in the running of the country.

REPUBLIC OF THE UNION OF MYANMAR

The country's name was changed to the Republic of the Union of Myanmar in October 2010, just prior to the general election that took place on November 7, 2010. The banned opposition party, the NLD, led by Aung San Suu Kyi, called on supporters to boycott the poll. This led to the forced dissolution of the NLD as it was split over this decision and under the election laws any party that chose not to take part in the polls had to disband. Many voters heeded opposition calls to boycott the election, with 25 percent of the seats in the national parliament and regional legislatures reserved for military appointees whatever the outcome. Over two-thirds of the 3,000 candidates were running for two parties that were both closely linked to the military junta. The main military-backed political party, the Union Solidarity and Development Party (USDP), says it won about 80 percent of the votes, although pro-democracy opposition groups claimed that the vote count was fraudulent. Even so the junta claimed that the election marked the transition from military rule to a civilian democracy.

A Myanmar worker displays the country's new national flag.

The election triggered fighting between ethnic Karen rebels and government forces, resulting in an estimated 20,000 people fleeing across the border to Thailand. To protest the government plan of incorporating ethnic armies into a centrally controlled border force, a faction of the Democratic Karen Buddhist Army (DKBA) occupied a police station in Myawaddy, which led to more fighting. Ethnic minority groups, approximately 40 percent of Myanmar's population, have been demanding greater regional autonomy since 1948, without much success. More than 1.5 million ethnic voters were disenfranchised in the 2010 elections because in some areas, deemed too volatile by the authorities, polling did not take place at all.

Many Western governments declared that the elections were neither free nor fair. Despite the storm of criticism some voters believe that the election could herald a modicum of change from the years of iron-fisted rule and economic mismanagement of the resource-rich nation.

INTERNET LINKS

www.cia.gov/library/publications/the-world-factbook/geos/bm.html

This site provides facts, figures, and dates relating to the Myanmar government, including administrative divisions, constitution, political parties, and leaders.

http://nobelprize.org/nobel_prizes/peace/laureates/1991/kyi-bio.html

This website includes a biography of Aung San Suu Kyi.

www.mofa.gov.mm/

The official website of the Ministry of Foreign Affairs, Naypwitaw, the Republic of the Union of Myanmar, contains links to foreign affairs, news, and information about Myanmar sections.

ECONOMY

A man selling flower garlands outside a Hindu temple in Yangon.

4

MYANMAR IS A LARGELY rural country with more than 75 percent of the population living in rural areas and over two-thirds of the civilian wage labor force of 24 million depend on agriculture for a living.

Roughly 7 percent are employed in industry and the remainder in services. Nearly half of the gross domestic product (GDP; a measure of a country's production) comes from the primary sector, including agriculture, forestry, fishing, and livestock rearing. About 25 million acres (10 million hectares) of land is cultivated out of a total of 45.5 million acres (17.25 million ha) of cultivable land; about 7.9 million acres (3.2 million ha) are rice fields.

A farmer plows the land. Most of the country is engaged in agriculture.

Myanmar is a resource-rich country that suffers from inefficient economic policies resulting in widespread poverty. Although the government has good economic relations with its neighbors, an improved political situation and a better investment climate are needed to promote exports, foreign investment, and tourism.

An Intha farmer plows his land with a hand-held tractor.

FARMING

Unlike in the West, in Myanmar farmers do not live on individual farms but in villages surrounded by fields. There are more than 14,000 village tracts in Myanmar. The farmers go out to the fields every day, where usually there are small huts for resting and eating. Although technically all land is owned by the state, farmers own the land they work for all practical purposes.

The main areas for rice growing are the Ayeyarwady delta, the coastal regions of Rakhine and Tanintharyi, and the Sittaung valley. Other areas also grow rice, but only for local consumption. Beans, pulses (seeds of leguminous plants), and oilseed are cultivated in the dry regions in central Myanmar and toward the northwest. Onions, chilies, and tobacco are also grown there.

The hill peoples cultivate many kinds of crops, but only for their own consumption and for barter because the terrain makes agriculture possible only on a limited scale.

Opium cultivation is said to form a substantial part of cash crop cultivation in the Shan State, but efforts are being made to encourage other types of cash crops, such as tea, coffee, and sunflowers.

OTHER OCCUPATIONS

Apart from agriculture the Myanmar engage in trading, manufacturing, and services. Such occupations are found mainly in the urban centers. In 2009 the labor force was estimated at 30.85 million. Of this number 70 percent were working in agriculture, 7 percent in industry, and 23 percent in services. The unemployment rate, estimated in 2009, stood at 4.9 percent. In 2009 the GDP was composed of agriculture (43.1 percent), industry (19.8 percent), and services (37.1 percent).

INDUSTRIES

The first modern factories in Myanmar, set up during the reign of the last two kings in the 19th century, were glass and steel factories, and a mint.

During the British colonial period, many industries such as rice-milling and petroleum refining flourished, but these were destroyed during World War II. After the war and after independence in 1948, industries were again established by many private entrepreneurs and by the government. Private entrepreneurs were active in the textile, food and beverage, and chemical industries, while the government was involved in pharmaceuticals, cotton, jute, and steel milling. During the 1960s private industries were nationalized by the government. Only very small private factories were left alone. In 1977 the Private Industries Law was passed; under this law, some industries, including those that produced food and beverages and clothing, were opened to private entrepreneurs.

The industrial policy of the socialist government was one of self-reliance, and efforts were made to establish industries that could substitute for foreign imports. There are more than 50 industrial parks in Myanmar, about half of them around Yangon. The Department of Human Settlement and Housing

Development (DHSHD) is developing industrial zones for local investors as well as foreign investors with the objective of creating more employment opportunities, and promoting urban development and technical knowledge and expertise. Some are reserved for state-owned factories, while others are being developed with foreign capital for foreign-owned enterprises or foreign companies that have entered joint-venture agreements with holding companies of the military government.

THE MARKET ECONOMY

Despite the country's efforts to industrialize, Myanmar's economy remains dependent on agriculture.

Since 1988 the SPDC regime has taken steps to reform its socialist economy into a market-type economy under the Union of Myanmar Foreign Investment Law, but the level and variety of investments are limited and the government has been reluctant to create open policies. The economy remains mainly under government control, despite claims of opening the economy. Many foreign investors who arrived in the country in the early 1990s have pulled out in recent years. In 1997 Myanmar was admitted to the Association of Southeast Asian Nations (ASEAN), which may have relieved international pressure against doing business in the country. However, later the same year, the U.S. government enacted restrictions against new investment in Myanmar by U.S. companies or citizens. In 2001 foreign investments under the liberalized regime of 1988 totaled about $7.4 billion. The largest investors are Singapore, the United Kingdom, Malaysia, and Thailand.

In 1996—97, annual foreign investment reached $2.6 billion and then fell to $29.5 million in 1997—98. The declining trend continued, and in the first half of 2002 investment from ASEAN members fell to zero. In 2003 the government introduced a measure that stopped the import and export permits to Myanmar-based foreign companies, making the regime even less attractive to foreign investors. The political standoff with Aung San Suu Kyi and her NLD party has also been a reason for investors to stay away; Aung San Suu Kyi herself asked investors to stay away from Myanmar, stating that their investments were likely to line the pockets of the ruling military. The human rights abuses alleged by international organizations such as Amnesty International have not helped to build investor confidence either.

Myanmar's export of teak and other hardwoods is an important component of its revenue.

In addition to the political climate, there remains the problem created by the overvaluation of the Myanmar currency in 2010 at 6.50 kyats per U.S. dollar whereas the real market value stands at 400 kyats or more per U.S. dollar. The banking system is also outdated.

Many economic reforms are still required for the Myanmar economy to be able to achieve a high growth rate. The average growth rate of the economy in 2009 was 4.4 percent.

SOURCES OF REVENUE

Myanmar's revenue comes from the export of primary products, mainly from the export of rice and rice products. During the British colonial period, Myanmar was the largest exporter of rice in the world, exporting an average of 3.3 million tons (3 million metric tons) annually. Total rice exports in 2009 and 2008 were 1.09 million tons (988,831 metric tons) and 547,600 tons (496,774 metric tons) respectively; the economic, social, and political problems of the past two decades have caused the decline in production. Nonetheless rice export earnings make up between 20 and 30 percent of total export earnings.

Besides rice another major source of revenue is the export of teak and other hardwoods. Myanmar produces about 90 percent of the world's genuine teak and is believed to have at least three-quarters of the total world reserves.

A woman works the loom in her village near Bagan.

Rubber, jute, corn, beans, sugarcane, mangoes, and pulses are also major export items, as are metals and minerals such as iron, tungsten, zinc, tin, and copper.

Myanmar is also famous for gems such as jade, rubies, sapphires, and cultivated pearls, which are sold every year at the Gems Emporium to foreign gem merchants.

Total export earnings for Myanmar in 2009 were about $6.845 billion.

WORK ETHIC

Traditionally Myanmar employers have looked after their employees with paternal care, while employees are expected to be loyal, faithful, and honest. Buddhist teaching stresses the learning of a craft or skill early in life as one of the necessary ingredients for success. Others are having good friends, spending modestly, and guarding possessions already acquired.

One of the main characteristics of the Myanmar at work is resourcefulness. Myanmar is full of examples of this: 50-year-old buses still run, as do old cars; many machines are run with locally made parts produced from lathe machines. The isolation of the country for almost 40 years has served to reinforce this trait.

Recycling was in existence in Myanmar long before the concept became popular in the West, but it is due to necessity rather than environmental concerns. Old newspapers, books, magazines, and exercise books have a ready market. Young children scrounge near garbage piles looking for scraps of plastic that can be melted down and made into new plastic bags. Old plastic buckets, basins, and baskets can similarly be melted and molded. Used oil drums can be used for storing water or rice. In households old bottles and cans are always saved to store sugar, salt, flour, and other kitchen ingredients. Car tires become rubber slippers.

Many private entrepreneurs have learned their business from family enterprises or from working as apprentices in other companies. They apply the skills they have learned and make ingenious adaptations rather than actual innovations. They are resourceful in spite of the restrictions that the private sector faces.

Public servants have few incentives to work hard since promotion is by seniority or the total number of years worked. They may moonlight or do some minor trading, sell food and clothing, or lend money at interest in order to stretch a low wage. Government wages were increased in April 2000, but the inflation rate is high and thus the increase in wages is insufficient to cover consumption costs. Many also turn to bribery; people who want quick attention from public departments have to put up with this practice. At the very least a favor is expected to be returned with another favor, and many departments work on this principle.

INTERNET LINKS

www.economywatch.com/world_economy/myanmar/

The Economy Watch website details economic, investment, and financial reports for Myanmar.

www.myanmars.net/myanmar-business/

This website provides information about business and the economy in Myanmar.

www.new-ag.info/country/profile.php?a=167

New Agriculturist, an online resource covering a wide range of stories and issues around rural development and agriculture across the globe, includes a country profile of Myanmar.

Phon Kan Razi National Park. Myanmar's beautiful and diverse environment is under threat by irresponsible logging, farming, and pollution.

5

THE MYANMAR ECONOMY HAS been deteriorating over the last few years and thus efforts to protect the environment, which include conservation of forests and underground minerals, have diminished. Fewer financial resources have been set aside for the protection of the environment as well.

According to statistics from the World Bank, Myanmar's population has also been living below the subsistence level. The World Bank has approved no new lending for Myanmar since 1987 and gave Myanmar the status of Least Developed Country of its 187 member countries in the same year.

Widespread poverty has led to excessive mining, harvesting, and extreme use of resources without regard for future generations' need for the same resources.

COMMERCIAL LOGGING

Deforestation has been caused by excessive logging of trees without replantation at an equal rate. Trees take a long time to reach maturity; for example, it takes about 100 to 150 years for a teak tree (*Tectona grandis*) to attain the girth that is commercially desirable. The foreign exchange that is needed to boost the economy is mainly brought in by the exports of teak and other hardwoods. These now take a prominent place over the rice exports, which had held up the economy

Myanmar has always been proud of its vast natural resources, which include land and forests, oil and gas, many kinds of gemstones, and underground minerals. Forty-eight percent of the vast country is forested. The forests include large stands of bamboo, hardwoods, and teak in the mountain ranges, and mangrove forests in the Ayeyarwady delta area.

since the British colonial years. Exports of timber brought in about $200 million in 2001–2002. Thus control of deforestation is not a priority and largely ignored.

In the 1970s and 1980s Myanmar had one of the lowest deforestation rates in Southeast Asia. Since 1988, however, the rate has doubled. Between 1990 and 2005 Myanmar lost 18 percent of its forest cover. The deforestation rate has increased by 13.5 percent since the close of the 1990s. Deforestation is also caused by the slash-and-burn type of shifting cultivation. This type of cultivation is used in small-scale agriculture. The farmers move from one place to another, each time clearing the land by felling trees and burning the scrub before they start to plant their crops.

Another reason for deforestation is the cutting down of trees for fuel, specifically for firewood. Myanmar has not had enough energy fuel for the growing population because of distribution and policy problems and poor infrastructure. As imports of fuel, production of oil, gas, and electricity were stopped owing to low foreign exchange reserves in 1997, the shortage problem has worsened in recent years.

Myanmar timber being transported for export. Myanmar is losing its forests at a rapid rate.

Forests are also cleared to make room for farmland.

Deforestation is one of the most destructive features of environmental abuse since it causes many ill effects on the environment. One negative side effect of deforestation is land erosion. Where the deforestation takes place on banks of rivers, the riverbanks may slide down to the riverbed and cause turbidity or muddy water. This in turn affects riverine life—the fishes and water plants and other flora and fauna living in the water of the streams and creeks. Turbidity also affects the lives of the people who depend on the river water for drinking and cooking and other purposes.

The rate of deforestation has been estimated by the Myanmar government to be at 2.1 percent per year, though independent bodies have said it is higher, at 6 to 8 percent. The rate has been accelerated by mechanical logging procedures. New roads were created by destroying more trees than when timber was extracted by using elephants and simpler equipment. Another factor causing accelerated deforestation is the opening up of some interior areas that had previously been inaccessible due to insurgent or rebel activities. The opening up of thickly forested areas came about because of the ceasefire agreements between the insurgent groups and the government.

The accessibility of the opened areas means that there are more hunters killing the wildlife living in these areas. Deforestation also causes changes in the migratory routes of many birds.

Among the most devastated areas are the mangrove forests in the Ayeyarwady delta. Deforestation has caused the delta to change shape, with more silting, greatly affecting the delta's marine life and the livelihood of the population.

One controversial economic venture has been the gas pipeline between Thailand and Myanmar, built to transport gas from the Gulf of Mottama gas fields. Clearing the massive areas of forests to make way for building pipes has generated much protest from environmentalists. Many villages of minority ethnic tribes are said to have been destroyed because of the gas pipeline. The habitats of fauna have also been destroyed in the process. The pipeline divided the terrain into two parts and caused dislocation for the fauna and people living in the area along the pipeline.

AIR POLLUTION

Pollution is more apparent in Yangon, where there are more cars and factories. Older cars have been moved to the outlying areas and provincial towns, but car exhaust fumes in downtown Yangon areas continue to be present at very high levels. Rules and regulations concerning exhaust emission are not being strictly enforced. Garbage disposal is also a problem in the inner city, with small back streets ending up as garbage dumps.

Self-sufficiency during the socialist period required investment in heavy industries, which caused much air pollution. In addition the continued use of obsolete equipment and machineries because of lack of capital to replace them with more energy-efficient and less polluting ones means that pollution of the environment will continue.

With the physical and population expansion of the capital, Yangon, owing to the large numbers of people migrating from the rural areas in search of better employment opportunities and a more modern lifestyle, Yangon can expect much more pollution if appropriate action is not taken soon. On the

Many farmers use slash-and-burn cultivation, which adds to the problem of air pollution.

other hand the entry of multinational factories and businesses that pollute the environment can also be expected with the opening up of the country unless agreements can be made from the start with these businesses, both local and foreign, regarding the protection of the environment, by the use of environmentally friendly equipment, proper waste disposal, and strict legal standards of pollution.

WILDLIFE

Myanmar has more than 1,700 known species of birds, amphibians, mammals, and reptiles according to figures from the World Conservation Monitoring Center. Of these 4.7 percent are endemic, and 5.9 percent are threatened. The region is one of the world's biodiversity hotspots; yet the decline of natural habitat through logging, pollution of rivers, and illegal trapping has caused the decline of many species. Commercial hunting, both

A baby elephant with its herd in Myanmar.

for local markets and for trade to China, threatens species. Tigers and turtles are among the species targeted for the wildlife trade. In 2010 a new monkey species, the snub-nosed monkey (*Rhinopithecus strykeri*), was discovered. But the single scientifically observed specimen had been killed by the time researchers found it in the remote mountainous Kachin state, and it was eaten soon afterwards. The bush-meat trade is just one of the pressures facing *R. strykeri*. Its habitat is being destroyed by logging companies. Scientists estimate that there are only about 300 of these monkeys remaining, few enough to qualify it for "critically endangered" status in the International Union for Conservation of Nature's Red List of Threatened Species. There are estimated to be 4,000 to 5,000 wild elephants and approximately 5,000 elephants in captivity in Myanmar. Trained elephants are still used in the logging industry, and although the government officially banned wild capture in 1994, it is known to continue to fulfill the needs of the timber industry.

LEGAL PROTECTION OF THE ENVIRONMENT

A number of environmental laws have been enacted, most of them after the 1988 demonstrations. Among the earlier acts are the Forest Act (1902), Wildlife Protection Act (1936), and Land Nationalization Act (1953); there are now also the Pesticide Law (1990), Forest Law (1992), and the Myanmar Mines Law (1994). There are other laws such as the Canal Act, Embankment Act, and Water Power Act, the Myanmar Marine Fisheries Law, Fresh Water Fishery Law, and Aquaculture Law. These laws are meant to protect the environment, but the government claims that enforcement of the laws is difficult because of the profit-seeking motives of private enterprises.

Enforcement of the laws would require the training and employment of a large number of rangers to protect the enormous areas to be covered, which include some very remote and inaccessible areas.

Myanmar regularly attends ASEAN meetings on the environment since the country became a member in 1997. Myanmar has entered a number of international and regional environmental agreements, including the United Nations Development Program's (UNDP's) Green House Gas Emission Reduction Plan in Asia.

Public education campaigns are required to raise awareness about the problems of environment that will impact future generations. There are at present few such campaigns.

INTERNET LINKS

www.eleaid.com/index.php?page=elephantsinburma

This site provides information and statistics on the wild elephant population of Myanmar, how its numbers are being depleted by the poaching of calves for export to Thailand, and how its habitat is being depleted by logging.

http://news.mongabay.com/2007/1014-burma.html

This article highlights environmental problems in Myanmar.

http://rainforests.mongabay.com/20myanmar.htm

This site provides an article and statistics on Myanmar forests.

www.wcs.org/where-we-work/asia/myanmar.aspx

The Wildlife Conservation Society website includes information about issues and projects in Myanmar.

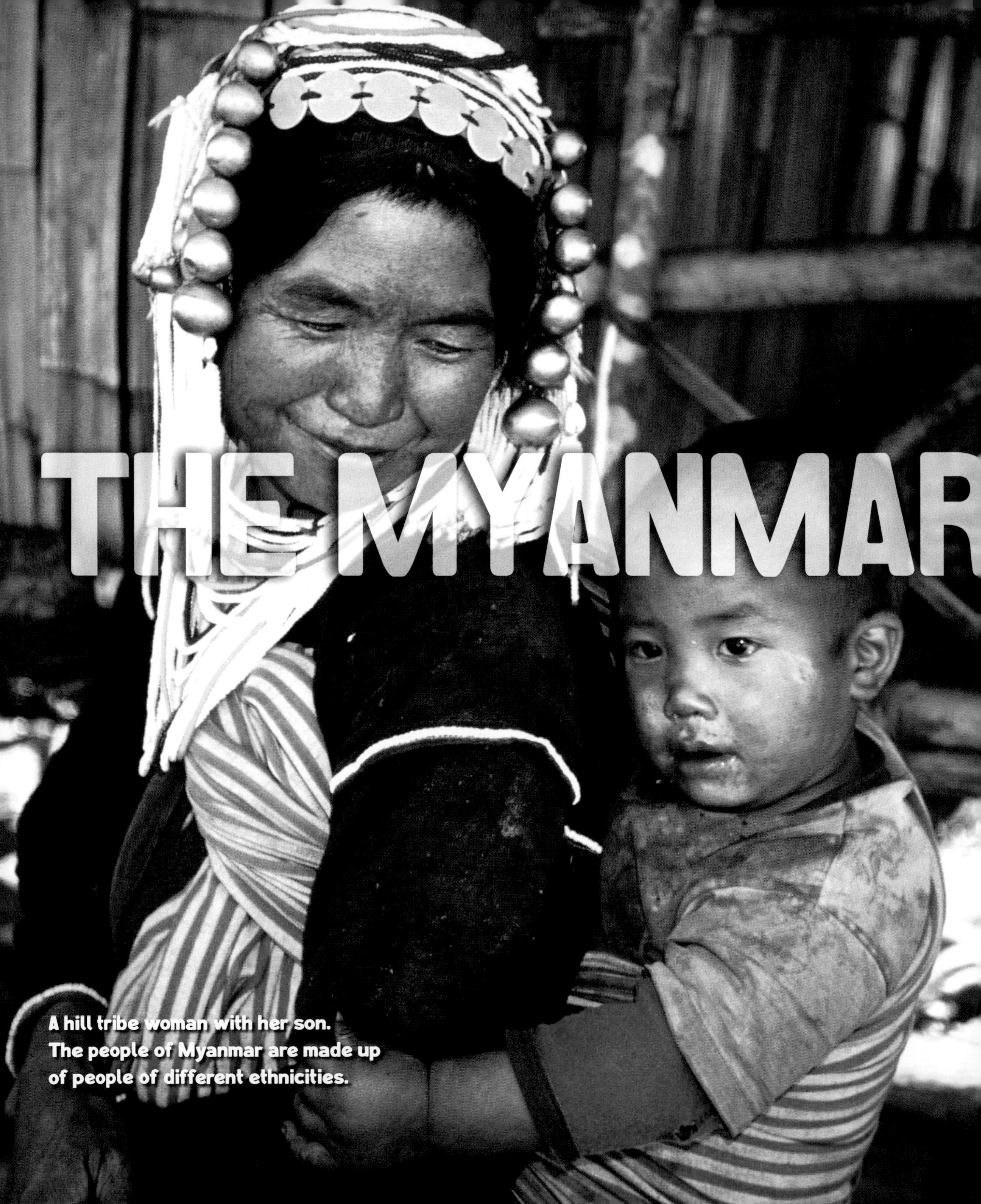

THE MYANMAR

A hill tribe woman with her son. The people of Myanmar are made up of people of different ethnicities.

6

The Myanmar have a deep respect for Buddhist monks and the elderly.

THE PEOPLE OF MYANMAR INCLUDE the ethnic Bamars and many different ethnic groups such as Kayin, Shan, Kachin, Kayah, Chin, Rakhine (Arakanese), Bamar, and the Mon. Although the people are generally known as Myanmar, there are distinct differences in customs and traditions among the ethnic groups.

SOCIAL HIERARCHY

Next to the Buddhist monks, the aged receive the most respect. A Myanmar family, however impoverished, does its best to care for elderly, disabled, or sick relatives, even those who are quite distantly related. Homes for the aged are homes for those who have no one to care for them.

Being educated is worthy of great respect, no matter whether one has gainful employment or not. Proud parents of university graduates line living room walls with photos of their offspring in their graduation caps and gowns. A foreign degree is generally regarded as superior to local degrees and diplomas.

Right: **A woman from Mon State. Each ethnic group has different practices and traditions.**

An Eng woman from the Shan State.

Among the professions, doctors and teachers are accorded high esteem. Doctors who practice for monetary fees alone are abhorred; they should be accommodating enough to accept their fees in kind, and people may pay them with items such as bags of rice or cans of cooking oil. Relatives and close friends are "looked after" free of charge by most doctors.

At the bottom of the hierarchy are those who live on the fringes of society—beggars, lepers, and cemetery dwellers, that is, people who have nowhere else to live. Most of these people are taken care of by government welfare and health institutions, but a few remain outside the network.

ETHNIC GROUPS

Myanmar has a diverse population, the result of three separate migrations from Central Asia and Tibet. The first migration brought the Mons and the Khmers. The second group of migrants consisted of the Tibeto-Bamars, and the third migration, sometime during the 13th and 14th centuries, brought Tai-Chinese peoples.

Bamars, or ethnic Myanmar, are the largest ethnic group, comprising about 60 percent of the total population. Referred to generally as Myanmar, as opposed to the other ethnic groups, they are descendants of the Bamars, Mons, and the Tai-Chinese; typically they are dark-complexioned and tall. Predominantly Buddhists, they live mostly in the river valleys and plains.

Closely related to the Myanmar are the Mons and Rakhine (Arakanese), who are also Buddhists and mainly farmers.

Kayins (Karens) are the third-largest ethnic group; Sgaw and Pwo Karens are the two main Karen groups. They live in the Ayeyarwady delta and also in hilly Karen State. They form about 7 percent of the population.

PADAUNG "GIRAFFE" WOMEN

A Myanmar lady had just arrived on a visit to London. As she unpacked her landlady stood nearby and kept looking at the articles being laid out. Finally unable to restrain herself, she asked the visitor, "Where are your neck rings?" This landlady's misconception was probably due to posters of Myanmar showing a Padaung woman with many copper rings around her neck. Actually the Padaung tribe numbers only a few thousand individuals who are seldom seen in the lowlands since they live in and around Loikaw, the Kayah State capital in east Myanmar. The rings are put on at an early age and increased year by year to a final total of about 20 pounds (9 kg)! This custom is said to be a deliberate deformation of the women of the tribe to prevent them from being taken by other tribes. The rings depress the collarbones and ribs and make the neck look unnaturally long. In fact the rings cannot be removed without substituting a neck brace, as the neck is weakened and there is a danger of suffocation otherwise.

Shan women on their way to the market.

The Shans, light-skinned and tall, are related to the Thais and the people of Laos, Cambodia, and Vietnam. Primarily farmers, they live in the river valleys and lowland pockets of the Shan plateau. They form 9 percent of the total population.

The Chin people live in Chin and Rakhine (Arakan) states. About 30 percent of the Chin have converted to Buddhism and Christianity; the rest are animists who worship spirits.

Kachins live in Kachin State in the northernmost part of Myanmar. They are well known for their fierce fighting spirit, as are the Chin people.

Kayah people were once known as Red Kayin (Karenni) and live in Kayah State, south of Shan State.

Apart from these main groups, there are many other smaller ethnic groups such as Palaung, Padaung, Lisu, Wa, Danu, Lahu, Lashi, Yaw, and others. The smaller ethnic groups tend to live in the more remote areas of Myanmar, although many have sought refuge in other countries.

DRESS

In place of pants and skirts, Myanmar men and women both wear sarongs called *longyi* (long-yee), but tie it differently; men knot it in front and women fold it to the side. The men wear a shirt, with a small stiff collar, tucked into the *longyi*. A jacket is worn over the shirt for formal occasions. Women wear over the *longyi* an *ainygi* (ayn-jee), a waist-length blouse with an overlapping flap in front. For weddings and important functions, they wear a net shawl over the blouse.

The *longyi* worn by the men is usually checked or striped, while the women wear *longyi* with more varied designs; they may be handwoven with traditional motifs or in single colors, or they may be made from imported materials in batik or floral prints. For formal occasions silk *longyi* are

THE VERSATILE *LONGYI*

The men's longyi *has all too often been a subject of curiosity because it resembles a skirt. Actually it serves many purposes: When crossing a stretch of water or climbing a tree a man can hitch it up, gather the front portion toward the back, between the legs, and tuck it in at the waist so it becomes short pants. It can be used to wipe a sweaty face; small articles can be carried in the front knot; and young children can sit on a father's* longyi *between his legs as in a hammock. Best of all it can be loosened after a big meal or to cool one's legs on warm days. Old worn* longyis *become rugs or cool sheets for babies to sleep on. Women can bathe with modesty at the riverside or village well by drawing their* longyi *up and wrapping it around the upper part of the body. The* longyi *keeps one's legs warm and free of mosquitoes, and sitting cross-legged is easiest in a* longyi.

essential for both men and women. Lace and brocade *longyi* are also worn by the women in the towns. Men sometimes wear a headgear called *gaung baung* (gaong-BA-ong) (*gaung* means "head" and *baung* means "wrapped around the head"), a close-fitting, brimless, silk hat with a loose piece at one side.

Younger girls nowadays prefer to wear Western-type blouses, or shirts, with a *longyi* worn calf-length, which is short to Myanmar eyes. Western dresses and skirts are also worn, but mainly in the capital city of Yangon and in Mandalay. Shorts, skimpy blouses and miniskirts are not approved of, generally speaking: The exposure of too much skin is considered indecent. For visits to monasteries and pagodas, Myanmar women take care to wear long sleeves and thicker materials.

For the Myanmar, footwear consists of a pair of thonged slippers, made of ordinary leather for everyday wear and velvet for special occasions. In the period after independence from the British, men wore shoes and socks on formal occasions, but in the ensuing socialist period that emphasized nationalism, slippers were the norm.

THANAKA

Thanaka (than-ner-kah) is a pale yellow paste applied to the face by Myanmar women and girls. The wood of several trees (collectively called thanaka trees) may be used to produce thanaka *cream. These trees include* Murraya paniculata *and* Limonia acidissima. *The cream is obtained by grinding a piece of the bark on a circular grinding stone with a few drops of water. This paste gives a cooling effect and reduces oiliness. Grandmothers love to apply from head to toe the large amount of* thanaka *prepared by granddaughters. Young girls working in the hot sun, transplanting rice seedlings by hand, apply thick layers to keep from getting too brown. Today it can also be bought in powder or lotion form.*

DRESS OF ETHNIC GROUPS

Although Mon and Rakhine peoples dress the same way as the majority of the Myanmar, the other ethnic peoples of Myanmar wear many different costumes in their own states. As more young people move to urban centers in search of employment, many have opted to wear the Myanmar dress of *aingyi* and *longyi*.

Karens wear a woven striped tunic over pants or *longyi*, and a scarf is tied around the head. Shan men wear loose black pants tied as a men's *longyi*, with a shirt, while the women wear a long-sleeved, tight, hip-length jacket and a *longyi*, and also a headscarf.

Kayah women wear a cape over their shoulders and a long sash. Kachin women wear thick woolen skirts, leggings, and black blouses decorated with silver disks and tassels, and the men wear black pants and shirts. Chin women wear a woven tunic and skirt with a long shawl over the shoulders. Palaung women wear blue jackets with red collars and skirts with bamboo hoops.

HAIRSTYLES

Men's hair used to be kept long and coiled into a topknot. In the colonial period men came to sport a short hairstyle called *bo-kay* (boh-kay), meaning "English-style hair."

As for the women their hairstyles have varied from dynasty to dynasty. Generally women are expected to have long hair after they reach adulthood and keep it rolled into a bun or chignon. They love to wear flowers at the side of their buns, such as a garland of jasmine or a rosebud. Fragrance is appreciated more than beauty, so the *thazin* (THE-zin), a delicate and tiny orchid, is highly prized for its haunting fragrance. Brides will pay a large sum to wear these flowers in their hair on their wedding day. Today young mothers, and even older women, prefer short hair, much to the dismay of their mothers.

INTERNET LINKS

www.myanmars.net/myanmar-people/

This website offers a comprehensive overview to the different ethnic groups that make up the Myanmar.

www.rohingya.org/index.php?option=com_content&task=view&id=101&Itemid=43

A site that highlights the plight facing the Rohingya people.

www.tourismmyanmar.com/dress.htm

Learn more about the unique traditional dress of the Myanmar.

LIFESTYLE

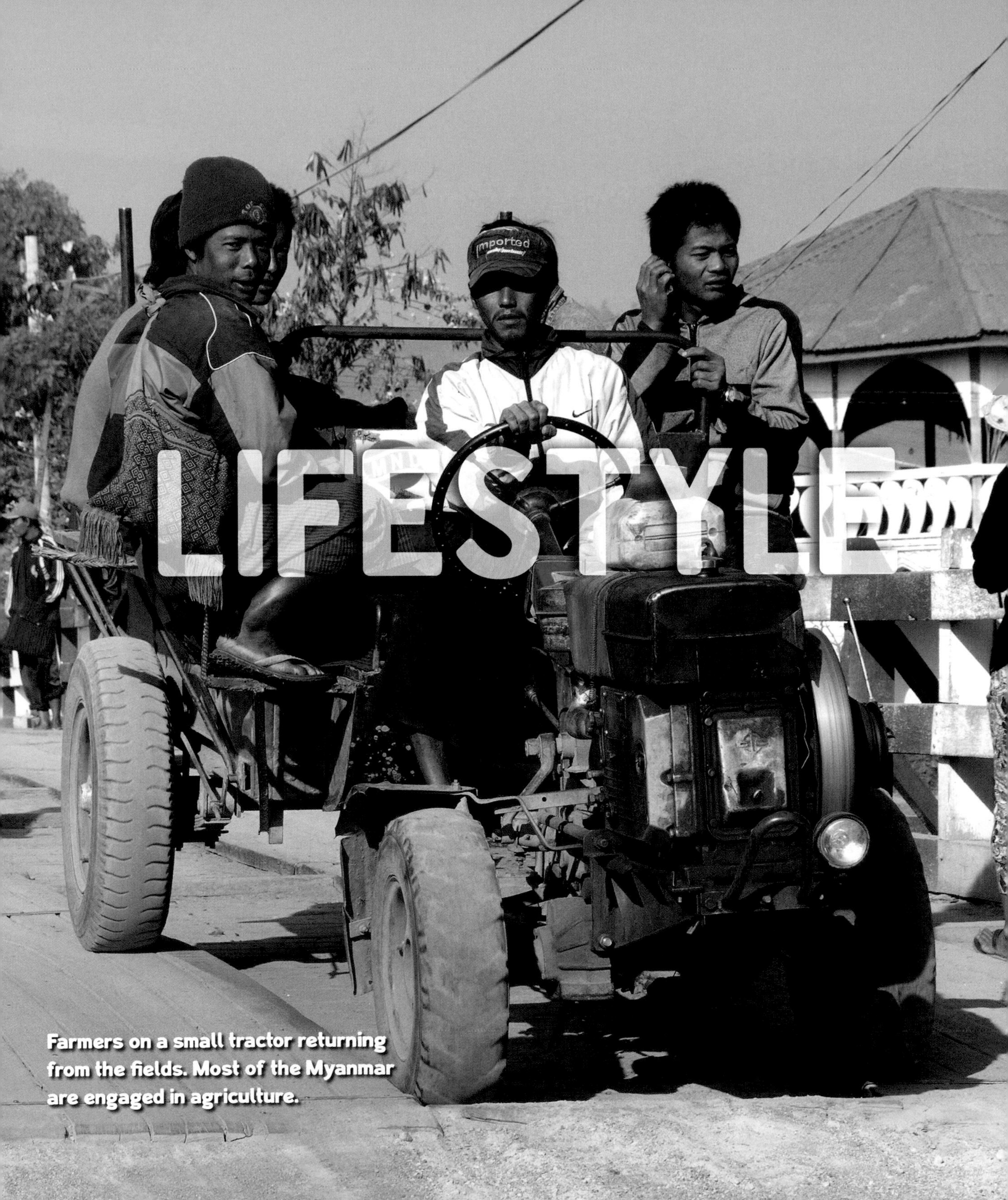

Farmers on a small tractor returning from the fields. Most of the Myanmar are engaged in agriculture.

7

THE MAJORITY OF MYANMAR ARE Buddhists and their attitudes and lifestyle are inevitably influenced by Buddhist beliefs. Buddhism plays an important role in the life of most Myanmar people from the cradle to the grave.

Although some Myanmar traditional cultures and beliefs have disappeared with the advent of modern influence and technologies, many are still highly valued and cherished by the majority of the people.

The lives of the Myanmar are influenced by their Buddhist beliefs and also their strong ties with their families. In contrast to urban life, the pace of life in rural areas is much slower.

ATTITUDES

A young child dies, the parents are grief-stricken, but they accept it as karma. A dishonest person gets cheated, a cruel person dies a gruesome death; this is the working of karma—reaping what one has sown. A Buddhist belief, deeply rooted in the Myanmar, is that everything that happens to a person, both good and bad, is the result of past deeds in the present and former lives. By the same token devout Buddhists know that any deed done in this life may affect their future rebirth. Myanmar Buddhists are afraid of *wut-ly-te* (woot-lai-tei), which means that evil deeds follow a person without fail, in this existence and others.

***Right*: A house on stilts in the stilt village of Ywama.**

Women making cheroots. Cheroot smoking is common in Myanmar.

Myanmar love a good joke and a tall tale, and are happy to spend a social evening around a pot of tea exchanging stories and anecdotes. Villagers are more carefree in that they do not worry so much about where their next meal will come from, since they have the trees and plants, and creeks full of fish on which to subsist.

In the towns life is not as easy: There are housing problems, and essential consumer goods such as rice, soap, meat, and cooking oil are expensive and not readily available.

AH-NAR-HMU

Ah-nar-hmu (AH-nah-hmoo), or *ah-nar-de*, is an important principle governing social relationships among the Myanmar and in their relationships with foreigners. It can roughly be defined as a feeling of hesitation in case one may be imposing a burden on another. An elderly aunt suffers in silence rather than telling her relatives that she is ill because she does not want to cause them the trouble of taking her to the doctor. A friend has borrowed some money and still has not returned it, but never will the lender ask for the borrowed money to be repaid.

Ah-nar-hmu results in white lies and beating about the bush, but most Myanmar are reluctant to cause another person trouble, loss of face, or hurt feelings. Western people, with their characteristic directness, are frustrated when they are unable to get a definite answer to a question, but this is mainly because most Myanmar always avoid giving a strong negative answer.

FAMILY

Family ties are strong among Myanmar. Buddhist tenets of the duties and responsibilities of parents and children are still closely followed. Parents expect obedience, and children have a duty to look after parents in their old age. The act of publicly disowning a child because of an unapproved marriage is not uncommon.

In many Myanmar families you will find grandparents, uncles, aunts, and cousins living under one roof. Privacy is minimal, all disagreements and quarrels are soon known, and there are always attempts at reconciliation on the part of the elders. Everyone is expected to help in his or her own way, either by contributing toward expenses; helping with cooking, washing, and other chores; or playing the role of advisor.

Myanmar are greatly supportive of relatives, and they include those close and distant, and even close neighbors, who are referred to as "relatives from the same block." Relatives from out of town will always stay with a family rather than go to a hotel. When there are no relatives to stay with, the Myanmar visitors prefer to stay in a monastery (after requesting permission of the chief monk). In Myanmar hotels are for foreigners.

In urban areas there are now many smaller families consisting of a couple, children, and perhaps a maid. Such parents do not receive the help and advice

A family poses for a photograph after a ceremony at Shwedagon Pagoda. The Myanmar have close contact with not just their immediate families but their extended ones as well.

A mother with her newborn baby at a clinic in Swe Kou Kou village.

of their own parents as in extended families; this sometimes leads to a lower quality of family life for all concerned.

BIRTH

Birth is an auspicious occasion in any family. To be without children is regarded as being pitiable.

The expectant mother is required to be careful in what she eats and does; here science and superstition appear to be well mixed.

In the villages pregnant women work in the fields or in home-based industries up to the last days before giving birth. Village midwives or elderly women attend to the birth. During the past decades government rural health centers and health assistants have been available, and traditional midwives have been gradually retrained. In the towns mothers receive free prenatal and postnatal care.

People in rural areas have large families because each child can later contribute on the farm. There is no strong preference for boys over girls since the birth of girls does not put a heavy burden on the parents with respect to dowry at marriage. Both boys and girls are accepted as gifts of "jewel children," meaning they are precious to their parents. Girls are expected to look after their parents, while boys are likely to be "given away" to the in-laws.

It was once the tradition to bury the umbilical cord at birth and to this day birthplaces are referred to as "the place where the cord is buried." The mother receives special care during the first days after delivery to clean her system, heal wounds, and make her strong again. Many callers come with gifts and good wishes to see the new baby.

COMMON PREGNANCY AND BIRTH TABOOS

The pregnant mother should not eat bananas, or the baby will be too big for normal delivery; chili, or the baby will have no hair; or glutinous rice, because this will make the placenta stick to the womb.

A pregnant woman should not attend weddings or funerals.

She should leave some things incomplete while pregnant, such as partially sewing baby clothes and leaving out the hems on the diapers.

After giving birth she should not wash her hair for about a month.

She should not eat bamboo shoots or mushrooms for some time.

She should not handle soap.

The child's name is chosen within a year. A ceremony may be held when the child's hair is washed with herbal shampoo, guests are invited, and all those who attend wish the child good health, wealth, and freedom from harm.

CHILDREN

Most Myanmar children have a carefree childhood. Parents are indulgent toward children, giving them what they ask for if or when they can afford it. Parents and grandparents may spoil them and excuse them for mischief, saying, "They are only children!" Parents often continue to look at their children as children and not as adults even after they are married and have children of their own.

Children are taken to most places and events except for funerals. They are given a lot of attention, admired, and never ignored. They are seen and heard. Parents seldom ask the children to go away while an adults-only dinner or conversation takes place. In any case the children soon get bored and will run away to play by themselves. In villages one can see young boys and girls smoking cheroots (rolled tobacco, much like a cigar) and no grownup will say anything.

Obedience is about the only thing that is expected of children. Buddhist teachings stress that when children grow up, they are obliged to look after their parents. When their parents die, children must make merits for their parents by donating money or gifts to monasteries. Merits are good deeds that lead to a better life now or in future existences.

In the villages or countryside, children climb trees, fish in the creeks, or go hunting in the forest. In farming communities the boys may help by tending the cows grazing in the pasture and collecting firewood; the girls help their mothers in the house with domestic chores or by looking after younger siblings. Children may go to the village monastery to learn basic Myanmar reading and writing or go to a government school. Often children living in the rural areas have to walk several miles for this purpose.

According to folklore, when a baby smiles, it is because, although jealous spirits taunt it by saying, "Your mother is dead," the baby knows this is untrue since it feeds at its mother's breast daily. When a baby cries, it is because jealous spirits say, "Your father is dead," and the baby, not yet knowing the father, believes them.

Today primary school enrollment rates are high and more schools are being constructed. However, less than half of all children in Myanmar currently complete primary school. Some school expenses must be paid by the students' families and this may be a financial obstacle. Most children in urban areas go to school; some children may be needed by their parents in the family business and have to stop their schooling after primary education (at

Children enjoying a game of tug-of-war.

about 10 or 11 years of age). Many children earn extra pocket money by selling cigarettes, tidbits, and other goods in the streets after school hours. In the towns children may be seen playing in the streets. They may fly kites, though this is dangerous in city streets.

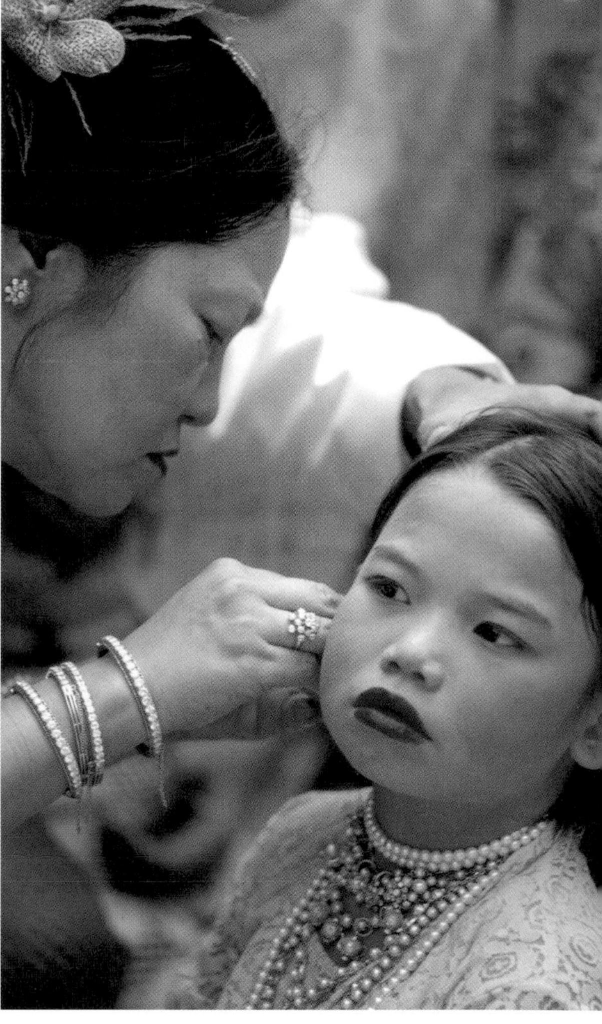

A young girl holds still during her ear-piercing ceremony.

PUBERTY

At about 12 or 13 years of age, the girls are gradually segregated from the boys: No more running around, climbing trees, or following the boys is permitted. They start to wear *longyi* and *aingyi*; no more bare legs are allowed. This may be one reason why Myanmar has so few sportswomen. Girls are also expected to keep their hair longer, although this custom is slowly dying out.

Girls are expected to behave more quietly than boys when speaking, laughing, and walking; that is, to behave with more decorum. Bathing at village wells or by the river is done in the company of other girls. Girls are expected to help their mothers around the house, and in rural Myanmar, their formal education generally stops at this age.

At puberty or sometimes earlier, young boys go through an initiation ceremony when they wear the yellow robes of a Buddhist novice for a short period at a monastery. This ceremony is held either for a single boy or a group of them, economy and convenience being taken into consideration. During the ceremony the boys' heads are shaved. Then they will put on monk's robes and stay at the monastery for a few days.

Some young girls go through an ear-piercing ceremony at the same time as their brothers and boy cousins become novices, but this ceremony does not have the same religious significance as the initiation. At this ceremony a girl will put on court dress and have her ears pierced and earrings put on.

Because of the great expense of feeding guests, this ceremony is seen much less frequently today.

Boys and girls brought up in the towns continue their education until grade 10, when there is a countrywide matriculation examination. They are about 16 to 18 years old at this time. If they pass this examination, they are able to pursue a university degree, and what they study depends on how well they do in the examination. Only those with very good results can go to medical and engineering schools.

In the 1990s the frequent closing of schools, colleges, and universities because of student unrest interrupted the education of many young people. Hence many students are graduating at a later age than before.

ROLE OF WOMEN

Women are regarded as inferior to men in the sense that they can never be ordained as monks or become Buddhas unless they are reborn as men. Women are not allowed to enter certain parts of religious buildings such as the middle platform at the Shwe Dagon. Socially, however, their status is equal to men; if they defer to men it is because of their own wish to give men the privilege of feeling superior.

Myanmar men are believed to have *hpon* (poh-n), or "glory," which is thought to be diminished if they touch women's skirts and underwear and other "unclean" articles. A man cannot prosper if his *hpon* is diminished. Some families wash men's clothing separately from the women's and also iron them with separate irons. Many women do their best to adhere to this practice.

In the family it is mostly the women who take charge of the household finances. Usually the husband hands over his paycheck to be used appropriately. Women also supplement the family income in many ways, such as running a small shop in front of the house, buying and selling various articles, setting up a small business making fruit preserves or cheroots, or acting as lenders of money or brokers for the sale of jewelry.

Professions such as teaching, accounting, and secretarial work are regarded by parents as suitable and proper for their daughters. As doctors most women become pediatricians or gynecologists because of the cultural segregation of the sexes and the taboo on touching between the sexes. Many women have broken into the ranks of lawyers and politicians that were for a long time the preserve of men.

Nursing was once the profession entered by Christian girls who were born to a religious code of kindness toward others and selflessness. In recent years many Myanmar women have entered this profession since it brings a good income and is meaningful. At a time when many with university degrees are unemployed, young girls in their late teens and early 20s are enrolling in nursing school instead of going to a university. Most parents, however, want a university education for their daughters, and a large proportion of university students is female.

Professions like teaching have been thought to be suitable careers for women, though this is beginning to change.

After marriage a woman keeps her own name. She may live with her parents or her in-laws. Deference is expected toward in-laws and parents, but it is not necessary for her to be around them at all times.

Although divorce is not very common in Myanmar, the estimated divorce rate is said to be higher than it was in the 1940s. When a couple is having difficulties in their marriage, the older members of the respective families try to help the couple work things out. If there is a divorce, the woman receives half of all property acquired after marriage and whatever she originally brought to the marriage. She can also freely remarry, whether she is divorced or widowed.

MARRIAGE

Beginning in their teens young girls and boys are generally segregated, but they have many opportunities to meet at village activities, in school, at the university, and at work as they grow into their 20s.

Portrait of a bride and groom in their wedding outfits.

Courtship customs among the Myanmar used to consist of writing love letters, initiated by the boy. In modern times the telephone has also been a means of communicating feelings. Dating usually takes place only when a girl has accepted a boy as a possible candidate for marriage. Groups of boys and girls may go out to tea shops or the movies.

Arranged marriages are still found among the Myanmar. Parents hope for a person with approximately the same ethnic background, economic status, and education for their child. A go-between, who may be a relative of either party, helps.

Marriages based on mutual love are also common, but parental approval is desired and sought. Where parents cannot agree to the marriage, relatives try to help in achieving a reconciliation.

Before World War II and after independence, eligible males were mainly those in the civil service, doctors, and engineers. This is still the case, but their ranks are now increased by merchant seamen who have gained social status due to their earning power in a deteriorating economic situation.

Engagements are not really necessary, but announcements can be made in the newspapers. A small ceremony may be held at the home of the bride-to-be with parents and relatives of both parties present. The qualifications and virtues of the bride- and groom-to-be are extolled by an elder who knows them well. Rings may be exchanged.

Marriage in Myanmar involves only the mutual consent of the two parties concerned. Living and eating together is enough to constitute marriage. Traditionally the marriage is valid if neighbors recognize it as such.

Weddings can be as simple or as elaborate as the parents and the couple wish. The simplest wedding is one held before a gathering of elders in the bride's home, the bride and groom sitting together on a smooth mat paying obeisance to the Triple Gems and their parents. Monks may be invited and offered alms. Other couples go to the court and sign a marriage contract before witnesses and a lawyer or judge.

The most elaborate weddings are held in Yangon's hotels, where several hundred guests are invited. They are entertained by a music troupe and well-known singers before the bride and groom are married in their presence. The marriage ceremony is performed by a master of ceremonies dressed like a Brahmin. The hands of the bride and groom are tied with a silk scarf and dipped in a silver bowl of water. Conch shells are blown and silver coins and confetti are scattered over the guests. Refreshments are served after the ceremony, usually tea with cakes, sandwiches, and ice cream. The bride and groom then go around and talk to the guests and accept congratulations.

Modern couples go on honeymoons to resort beaches or to highland resorts such as Pyin oo lwin (Maymyo) and Taunggyi.

DEATH

To the Myanmar death is accepted as just one stage in the life cycle. The dead person is simply leaving his or her body behind to move on to a new rebirth. From the Buddhist perspective death is never seen as the end. From the Buddhist perspective birth is not the beginning and death is not the end. It is just one part of a whole process, a whole cyclic process of birth, death, rebirth, dying again, rebirth, dying again. Conditioned by the moment of death is rebirth. The family grieves, but not for a long period of time. No mourning periods are specified.

When a person dies while away from home—for example, on the way to the hospital—the body is not allowed back into the village or street quarter. It is common to see a corpse in its coffin laid out for burial just outside the village boundary.

On the day a person dies, the family invites a monk to the family's monastery and makes an offer of food to indicate that a life has been lost. The dead person is bathed and dressed in his or her favorite clothes. Candles, incense sticks, water, and token offerings of food are placed at the head. An earthen water pot is placed under the bed on which the body is laid.

The spirit of the dead person is believed to be still in and near the residence up to a week after death. There is a wake that lasts a whole week. Doors and windows are kept open throughout this period. In villages all the villagers help. The youths help by staying awake through the night and letting the family members, exhausted by grief and by talking to callers the whole day, take a rest. The young people stay awake by playing cards, drinking plain tea, and eating snacks. Other neighbors assist in cooking the food for the family and other helpers.

A week later monks are invited again to be given alms, to pray, and to remind the spirits of the deceased that they are no longer members of the household and must go their own way. All merits are shared with them in order that they might be reborn to a better life.

At the funeral the height of each member of the family is measured with thread; the lengths of thread are then put into the coffin. A 25-*pya* (piah) coin

A cemetery in Nyaungshe.

is placed in the mouth of the deceased to be used as payment to the ferryman when crossing to the land of the dead. The water pot is broken. The grief of the bereaved reaches a climax, and there is no restraint in weeping and lamenting; it is believed that the relief of crying is healthy for the bereaved. Burial is usual in Myanmar, but in Yangon cremation is common. The ashes of the dead are usually not collected after cremation as they are among other cultures.

Among the ethnic groups, the Buddhist Karens living in the Kayin State perform a bone collection ceremony a year after death. The bones of the dead are collected and placed in a special hut, and food and prayers are offered.

In the villages very simple markers are used for graves, and there is generally no effort to maintain graves or to celebrate a day such as All Souls' Day. Instead the dead are remembered at feasts offered to monks for the purpose of sharing merit with them. Many other good deeds, such as donations to homes for the aged, donating scripture books, building monasteries, and food offerings, may be done by the remaining members of the family to help the dead on their way along the cycle of existence.

INTERNET LINKS

www.unicef.org/myanmar/index.html

The United Nations Children's Fund (UNICEF) has been working in Myanmar since the 1950s. This website has links to many different aspects of the work.

www.myanmar.com/lifestyle/index.html

This site provides information on lifestyle and activities, including traditional medicine, food, toys, and games.

www.myanmars.net/myanmar-people/

This site describes Myanmar peoples and lifestyles, including history, language, culture, and photos.

RELIGION

Two Buddhist nuns pray at the Shwedagon Golden Temple.

8

BUDDHISM IS THE PREDOMINANT faith in Myanmar, but other religions exist and there is full freedom of worship.

BUDDHISM

Ninety percent of Myanmar's population is Buddhist; this includes about 99 percent of the Myanmar, Shans, and Karens. The form of Buddhism practiced in Myanmar is Theravada Buddhism, similar to that found in Thailand, Laos, Sri Lanka, and Cambodia, and different from the Mahayana Buddhism of China, Japan, Korea, Tibet, Nepal, and Vietnam.

Monks collecting alms are a common sight in Myanmar.

Myanmar is a predominantly Buddhist country, with Buddhism of the Theravada school being practiced by nearly 90 percent of the population. Other religions practiced in Myanmar include Christianity, Islam, and Hinduism. Buddhism plays a vital role in daily life and many Buddhist rituals are incorporated into people's daily routine.

THE FOUR NOBLE TRUTHS

The Four Noble Truths discerned by the Buddha upon reaching enlightenment are, first, that all life involves pain—suffering, birth, disease, old age, and death. No matter how wealthy one may be, one cannot escape any of these ills. Second, the reason for these ills is craving, desire, or attachment to things, pleasures, and people. Third, detachment can bring an end to pain and an escape from the cycle of rebirths. Fourth, detachment can be achieved by following the Eightfold Path.

The Lord Gautama Buddha was not a god but a human being, a prince of a kingdom in India who lived more than 2,500 years ago. He renounced the material world at the age of 29 to look for a cure for the ills of the world, including disease, old age, and death. He practiced various methods for a period of six years until he gained enlightenment, having understood the Four Noble Truths and found the Middle Way, or Eightfold Path, a guideline to escape from the sufferings of all people.

Buddhist devotees presenting offerings and praying at the Shwedagon Pagoda.

THE EIGHTFOLD PATH

The Eightfold Path consists of right understanding, right thought, right speech, right action, right livelihood, right effort, right mindfulness, and right concentration. There are strict definitions of what constitutes "right": Right speech, for example, means refraining from empty chatter, gossip, and abuse.

BUDDHIST PHILOSOPHY The basic philosophy of Buddhism is that the universe and all forms of life in it are in a constant process of change, from birth to death. After death there is rebirth; the cycle of death and rebirth is endless until Nirvana (nir-vah-nah) is reached. Nirvana is defined as an extinction of greed, anger, and delusion (belief in ego or self). There are 31 planes of existence into which beings can be born depending on their karma, which is the result of their thoughts, deeds, and speech. Some of these planes of existence are the animal plane, the ghost planes, the human plane, and the celestial planes.

A mother and child praying at a shrine.

The law of karma is a law of cause and effect: Whatever happens to one is the result of one's past actions—including thought, deeds, and speech—in previous existences, and one can expect to reap the result of one's actions in this life or future lives. The ideal goal of a Buddhist should be to reach Nirvana and make a complete severance from the cycle of existences. The way to reach Nirvana is to acquire morality, concentration, and wisdom, or insight, by following the Eightfold Path.

BUDDHIST WORSHIP The Buddhists worship the Triple Gems that are the Buddha; the Dhamma, or his teaching; and the Sangha, or his disciples, the monks. The Dhamma, which means truth or law, consists of the scriptures known as the *Tripitaka* (Three Baskets). Buddhists cannot ask the Buddha for fulfillment of wishes. They do all they can to gain merit by keeping the five precepts of abstaining from killing any living beings, stealing, adultery, lying, and taking intoxicants; and occasionally, the eight precepts that include celibacy, avoiding entertainment and adornment, and sleeping on

The main Buddha image in the Sandamuri Pagoda.

Muslims listening to a teacher. Despite Buddhism being the dominant religion, believers of other religions are able to practice their faiths without fear.

luxurious beds. These are only the fulfillment of morality. For wisdom and concentration they have to practice meditation in any one of 40 methods.

OTHER FAITHS

Buddhists form the majority of the population in Myanmar, but there are also Christians, Hindus, Muslims, Chinese Taoists, Confucians, Jews, and animists.

The earliest conversions to Christianity took place around the early 17th century. A significant number of Karens, Chin, Kachin, and Myanmar are Baptists. Christian missionaries were active from the colonial period up to the mid-1960s, establishing schools and running hospitals and social welfare centers, which were of high standards and provided good-quality services. After 1962 these establishments were nationalized by the government.

PLACES OF WORSHIP

To a visitor every hilltop in Myanmar appears to have a pagoda on the summit, even if it is small and only whitewashed. Myanmar has often been called the

Land of Pagodas. Even Mount Victoria, Myanmar's third-highest peak, has a pagoda on its peak, 10,150 feet (3,093 m) up. Pagodas are usually built high up since they contain holy relics and therefore should never be on a level lower than people's houses.

Pagodas are solid conical structures with a central treasure vault below. A terrace around the pagoda provides pilgrims with space for praying, meditating, or making offerings. Temples are built with a hollow chamber in the center unlike pagodas, and pilgrims can enter the temple. Other Buddhist structures include Buddha images built in the open or under a shelter. A *Dhamma-yone* (Der-mah-yohn) is a place where sermons and feasts are held.

Entrances to large pagodas and temples are lined with small stalls where people sell flowers and sprigs of leaves, candles, gold leaf, small paper umbrellas, streamers, and fans to be offered to the Buddha. It is customary to remove shoes and slippers when entering these places, as a sign of respect. Myanmar women wear a brown shawl or scarf that is wrapped around one shoulder across to the waist when they pray.

Aerial view of Shwezigon Pagoda. Pagodas are common features in most of the temples in Myanmar.

Monasteries are places where monks reside, but people may also go there to pay their respects and offer alms of food and provisions, money, and robes. They may spend a whole day or several days at a monastery observing the precepts and meditating in one of the *zayat* (zer-YAHT), meaning "resting place," in the grounds. Many religious feasts, including those for novitiation and robe-offering ceremonies, are held in monasteries. Women are forbidden to enter some parts of a monastery.

Every Buddhist household has a shrine in the living room, either built into a wall or placed on a high table or cupboard. Images of the Buddha, some of which may have belonged to ancestors, are placed together with images of the Buddha's disciples and pictures of famous pagodas, monks, and relics. Daily votive offerings that are consecrated in fulfillment of a vow may include flowers, candles, water, and food.

In Myanmar faiths other than Buddhism are also freely worshiped and one can find churches, cathedrals (such as the famous Holy Trinity and Saint Mary's), mosques, Hindu temples, and Chinese temples in Yangon and many other towns in the country.

HOLY SYMBOLS AND RELIGIOUS RITES

Myanmar Buddhists show reverence to the Buddha by keeping the Buddha's image in their household shrine and offering flowers, candles, water, and food. The food is a token portion from a newly cooked pot of rice, a new cake, or fruit just bought and washed. The food is offered at dawn or in the early morning and thrown away at noon. Flowers are changed as they wither, and water is changed daily. The Buddha's image is a visual aid that reminds the Buddhist that the Buddha really lived over 2,500 years ago and was a supreme human being. It confirms a person's confidence or belief in the teaching of the Buddha.

Buddhists hold their palms together in reverence when they pass a pagoda or meet monks. Pagodas are sacred because most of them contain relics of the Buddha inside their central vault. Books and pictures of the Buddha are also sacred; these should never be placed underfoot or stepped over. Buddha

Buddhist devotees presenting offerings at a shrine in a temple.

images should never be lower than head level. It upsets Buddhists to see images of the Buddha placed at the foot of stairs as decoration, inside bookshelves, and even used as umbrella stands.

The banyan tree is holy because it is the tree under which the Buddha reached enlightenment; banyan trees are seldom cut down. Small shrines are built on their trunks, and flowers and candles are offered. Drooping branches of the banyan are sometimes propped up with bamboo poles to earn merit for a sick or dying person.

When misfortune comes to a family, it is common to invite monks to the home, offer them alms, and request them to recite the *paritta*, or scriptures, which are believed to have the power to overcome dangers, disease, and misfortune. Flowers, water in a bowl, sand, and spools of thread are placed before the monks. After the recitation the water may be drunk as holy water, the sand sprinkled around the outside of house, and the thread cut up whenever necessary and tied around objects in the house or around the wrists of children to ward off evil.

After prayers a devotee beats a small triangular gong with a small wooden mallet or rings a bell as a symbol of sharing merit with all beings.

A 24-petaled chrysanthemum is the symbol of the *Paticca-samuppada*, the Law of Dependent Origination, one of the topics preached by the Buddha, and sometimes used to symbolize Pathana, the 24 Causal Relations, the 24 modes or relationship within the group of cause and effect.

The Law of Dependent Origination is one of the important Buddhist laws of the universe discovered through enlightenment. It is an elaboration of the principle of cause and effect; in other words, one reaps what one sows. Every effect has its cause. The law states that:

It is produced; therefore the other is produced
It is extinguished; therefore the other is extinguished.

It exists; therefore the other exists.

It does not exist; therefore the other does not exist.

Golden umbrellas are placed on hearses of those who have built pagodas and monasteries during their lifetime.

FOLK BELIEFS

In spite of centuries of Buddhist practice, animism—the worship of spirits that has existed from an even more remote time—continues to exist alongside Buddhism. Ghosts and demons have not been seen by many, but that is no reason to disbelieve those who claim to have seen them.

The Myanmar spirit world has 37 *nats*, or spirits. Most of these are spirits of those who have died a violent death. Shrines are built for them and offerings are made. Most of these spirits are appeased out of fear, for they are capable of punishing more than rewarding. That does not mean, however, that one cannot ask them for health, fame, or fortune.

Even among those who have given up animistic worship, a spell of bad luck and a visit to an astrologer can make them revert back to their traditional spirit worship to appease spirits that still want their offerings.

For nat worship, it is the custom to hang a green coconut in a small basket in a corner of the living room. If there is an illness, for example, and the stem of the coconut is found to be dry, it is assumed that the spirit is angry because the coconut has not been replaced by a fresh one. Those who work on the stage, make movies, or play in orchestras customarily need to offer bananas, coconuts, and tobacco leaves to the spirit of the arts before performances.

Cursing for a person to die, even in jest, is frowned on; statements such as, "Bye-bye, I'm going and not coming back again," and similar words are believed to be omens of death and bad luck. Children are admired, but one should never say how fat, tall, or healthy they are in case the spirits get jealous and make them sick. Nor should one say, "I never get sick, never catch a cold." Wives should not wash their hair when their husbands are away. Hair should not be washed or cut on Monday, Friday, or the day of one's birth. Hair should not be washed in the evenings or let down loose after dark. Pots should not be banged with ladles, as this may invite hungry ghosts. Clothes should not be put on back to front during play (because corpses are dressed this way). Children should not hide inside rolls of mats.

Woodcutters and hunters who live off the jungle are very careful with their language so as not to anger forest spirits. Fishermen and miners have their own spirits to worship. Some places are believed to have particularly powerful spirits, and visitors are warned not to anger them by making jokes or belittling them, as they can make one lose one's way and cause other trouble. One should never say, "Come along, everyone," when passing cemeteries, because ghosts may follow.

Because the belief in rebirth is widespread, Myanmar children born with peculiar traits will draw comments regarding their previous existence. Similarly an animal that exhibits human-like characteristics is said to be "close to human existence." There are many stories of people who are reborn in neighboring villages (they have mannerisms or traits of those who have died), and those who are able to recall their previous lives.

MAGIC

Black magic or sorcery is widely believed in, especially in villages. Villagers may be afraid of someone who seems to possess magical powers. Spells may be cast on children and adults, sometimes not out of malice or anger but out of love. Bad spells can be cured by those who have the power to undo the spell and punish the perpetrator. These people are not monks but they lead virtuous lives in order to possess the power to drive away evil spirits. They give charms such as holy thread and holy water, or make offerings to prevent or break a spell. A spell may manifest itself in illness or strange behavior that cannot be cured by conventional medicine. If a person dies and a spell is suspected, it is usual to cremate the body; the spell is said to remain unburned in the ashes.

Spells may be hidden in food, which is then fed to unsuspecting victims, or they may be buried in the victim's garden or under the house. These spells, called *inn*, are pieces of slate, wood, bone, or foil on which squares are made and filled in with letters or numbers. The very same kind of *inns*, but "good" ones, are dispensed by astrologers to deflect any bad luck. The squares are placed on altars, and lit candles are placed on them.

Besides "magicians," clairvoyants, astrologers, and palmists abound in Myanmar. They are consulted by those who wish for certainty at some point in their lives. When a clairvoyant's powers become known, people line up at the doorstep to learn about their own future.

Astrologers are consulted to pick auspicious days for weddings or groundbreaking ceremonies or identify days on which to be cautious. To change the luck of a person, an astrologer may offer a change of name or advise offering certain flowers and leaves to the Buddha. He may advise on the kind of merit one should make; for example, the number of birds and fishes to set free, the number of rounds of rosary to say, or the kinds of food to avoid.

Astrologers and palmists may be found on the streets and on pagoda grounds. Large posters and big banners announce their names and advertise their claims of being able to predict winning numbers in the state lottery, a marriage partner, and even future existences.

INTERNET LINKS

www.myanmartourmandalay.com/festival.htm

This site provides details of annual traditional Myanmar religious festivals.

www.burmalibrary.org/docs/ITBMU.htm

This website contains images of Myanmar: a year at the Theravada Buddhist Missionary University in Yangon.

www.accesstoinsight.org/lib/authors/bischoff/wheel399.html

This site provides a short history of Buddhism in Myanmar.

LANGUAGE

A man reading a magazine in Pansodan Lan.

9

THE MYANMAR LANGUAGE BURMESE belongs to the Tibeto-Bamar language group, which is a subfamily of the Sino-Tibetan family of languages. To a foreign ear Burmese sounds much like Chinese. It is monosyllabic and tonal; mispronunciation of tones results in meaningless sentences. Burmese is the official language in Myanmar.

Although it is officially recognized as the Myanmar language most English speakers continue to refer to the language of Myanmar as Burmese. It is the native language of the Bamar and related sub-ethnic groups of the Bamar as well as some of the ethnic minorities in Myanmar such as the Mon. It is spoken by approximately 32 million people as a first language.

SPOKEN LANGUAGE

Spoken Burmese differs from region to region; some regional accents are quite strong. In regions such as the eastern state of Rakhine (Arakan),

A young boy reads a textbook during an elementary school class.

FIRST ENGLISH-BURMESE DICTIONARY

The first English-Burmese dictionary was compiled during the middle of the 19th century by Adoniram Judson (1788—1850), an American Baptist missionary. Judson had arrived in Myanmar in 1813. In 1824, during the second Anglo-Myanmar war, he was imprisoned with other foreigners in the capital of Innwa and was released a year later.

Judson completed the English-Burmese dictionary in 1849; a Burmese-English dictionary remained unfinished at the time of his death. It was completed only in 1852 by another missionary, Edward Oliver Stevens. These two dictionaries are still in use today.

Muslim students in school. Most Myanmar are able to speak, or at least have a grasp of, English.

and Dawei and Myeik in the south, the dialects spoken are forms of old Burmese.

The young people in Myanmar may use many slang words within their speech, which is frowned upon by the older people as being coarse and decadent. However, slang continues to be popular among the younger generation, and its usage is reinforced by comic books, cartoons, novels, and popular songs.

Because Myanmar was once a British colony, most Myanmar can speak, or at least understand, simple English. Those Myanmar who were of school age during the Japanese occupation are able to speak simple Japanese.

The ethnic groups speak their own languages. Most Myanmar are unable to speak the ethnic languages, but many ethnic groups have learned to speak Burmese. Myanmar script has its origins in Brahmi script, which flourished in India from around 500 B.C. The Kachin, Chin, and Kayin have Romanized alphabets developed by the early missionaries. The Shan and Mon also have their own writing.

NICKNAMES

Nicknames are quite common, especially in childhood. These nicknames are given in the spirit of love and humor; a very dark child might be called Maung Mai, *or "Master Blackie." Some nicknames are deliberately demeaning—a very sickly child may be called* Maung Than Chaung, *or "Master Iron Bar," just so that he might grow stronger and sturdier.*

In many families the children are nicknamed by their position in the family: Ko Ko *(big brother),* Ma Ma *(big sister),* Nyi Nyi *(younger brother), and* Nyi Ma Lay *(youngest sister).*

FORMS OF ADDRESS

For the Myanmar, how one addresses or speaks to a person depends on his or her age and social status. When addressing monks, one must use a special form of speech. Elders, teachers, doctors, and those worthy of respect are addressed in polite form. Honorific titles must be used with such persons, while among equals—in age or social status—a freer form of speech is used. *Ko* and *Daw* are used for addressing adult men and women, respectively; *Maung* is used for younger men, and *Ma* for young women. *Saya* is used for teachers, doctors, or one's employer; *sayama* is the feminine form.

MYANMAR SCRIPT

The Burmese alphabet consists of 33 letters that are combined with various symbols to indicate the tones. The letters are circular in appearance. These letters were originally square, derived from rock-cut scripts of south India, but have gradually become rounded because the traditional palm leaves used for writing would have been torn by straight lines.

Although the alphabet was derived from the Pallava script of South India, which itself was based on the Brahmi script, it did not come directly from the original source. The Myanmar obtained their alphabet from the Mons of

A roadside stall offering a typing service.

ancient Thaton, who had earlier received religious teachings in Pali, possibly from the fifth-century Buddhist center in Kanchipuram (Chennai), in the southern part of India.

MYANMAR NAMES

Myanmar names are not structured in the same way as names in most other countries. Internationally most people have a two- or three-part name, first (given) name, middle (given) name, and last name (family or surname). So a girl's name may be Elizabeth (first name) Mary (middle name) Poole (surname or family name). The surname is carried down from the father's side of the family. These names do not change throughout a person's life, and every single document relating to a person will have the same name. In Myanmar surnames do not exist at all, and a child could be named by using a system in which each day of the week is assigned letters of the alphabet. The name is chosen by using the letters that belong to the day the child was born.

OLD BURMESE MANUSCRIPTS

In the past the Myanmar wrote on paper, lacquered boards, and palm leaves. Parabaik, or concertina manuscripts, are made from crude strong paper made out of mulberry or bamboo pulp. Parabaik manuscripts may be 8 feet (2.4 m) long and 18 inches (46 centimeters) wide and folded like a concertina, each fold being about 6 inches (15 cm) long and 8 inches (20 cm) wide. Palm-leaf manuscripts, or pay-sar*, are made out of dried palm leaves that are trimmed, sewn, and folded, and written on with a metal stylus. Religious, literary, and scientific works, letters, and horoscopes were in the form of palm-leaf manuscripts. Burmese Buddhist palm-leaf manuscripts, or* kammavaca*, contain Buddhist scriptures in Pali, written in a square script of black lacquer on gold leaf.*

ASTROLOGY AND NAMES

Names may also be chosen based on the advice of an astrologer or a monk. Astrological calculations are made and a name is chosen that is designed to reduce negative aspects and bring good luck to the child. People may even change their name on the advice of an astrologer at a later date simply by choosing a different name. So a Myanmar person could have many different names, and those names could change throughout life. The only way to find out a person's background and family is to ask who the parents are, where they live, where they work, and so on until identity can be established.

NONVERBAL LANGUAGE

Although the Myanmar are an informal people they consider it very important to show respect to elders and those of a higher social status not only in the use of speech but also in gestures and posture. If an older person is sitting on a mat, it is not acceptable for a younger person to be sitting on a chair, and if the younger person wants to speak to the

CHOOSING A NAME THE MYANMAR WAY

Letters assigned to the different days of the week are:

Monday — ka, kha, ga, nga
Tuesday — sa, hsa, za, nya
Wednesday — wa, la, ya, ra
Thursday — pa, pha, ba, ma
Friday — tha, ha
Saturday — ta, hta, da, na
Sunday — a, e

U Ba Khin (Thursday-born) and his wife Daw Khin Khin (Monday-born) might name their Friday-born daughter Ma Thet Thet. Care has to be taken in picking the name since certain combinations of letters are supposed to be favorable and others bring bad luck to a person.

older person on the mat the younger person must bow slightly from the standing position. Similarly a younger person should bow slightly when walking past an older person. When walking past a pagoda or a meeting a monk, the palms of the hands are held together as a show of reverence. It is disrespectful to pass an object over the head of an older person. When passing an object to an older person, respect is shown by holding the left hand at the right elbow.

The *kadawt* (ker-dorht) gesture is used by the Myanmar to show respect or gratitude to parents, grandparents, teachers, or anyone of higher social status. One crouches down to the floor, with palms held together, and touches the floor with the elbows and head. This gesture may be carried out when a person is going away, or to show gratitude for a favor received. It is also used to show respect when someone has died.

A person's feet are considered the lowliest part of the body, but the head and hair are held reverent. An office worker will never put his feet on the

MYANMAR SMILE

A smile in Myanmar may be used to convey any number of expressions depending on the circumstance and moment. People smile at each other in greeting. But a smile could equally convey anger, sarcasm, shyness, amusement. A Myanmar student in England would smile at his professor every time he passed him. The smile was meant as a greeting. But one day the professor looked at the student, rather puzzled, and asked, "Am I very funny?"

desk, and to kick someone is not only considered aggressive but extremely rude as well. As a sign of respect and reverence, footwear is removed when entering a Myanmar home or any religious building.

Women are accorded equal status with men, but they are not permitted to enter certain places, such as the higher levels of a pagoda. At religious congregations and ceremonies women sit apart from men.

Women's garments are never hung out to dry in front of a house or overhead. Public shows of affection are considered an embarrassment. Touching is taboo between the sexes even within a family group.

INTERNET LINKS

www.wholesomewords.org/biography/biorpjudson.html

This site provides short biographies on the American Baptist missionary Adoniram Johnson, along with related links.

www.thenatureactive.com/myanmar-name/

This website details the structure of Myanmar names.

www.myanmars.net/myanmar-language/

This site describes the Myanmar language, including links to proverbs, scripts, poetry, and literature.

ARTS

A local artist puts the finishing touches on her lacquerware creation.

10

Myanmar is a country full of ancient traditions and culture, but historically Myanmar art has been heavily influenced by Buddhism. The 10 Myanmar traditional arts, metaphorically known as "Ten Flowers," have been passed down through the centuries.

AS WITH MANY ASPECTS of Myanmar life, the arts are closely tied to the Buddhist way of life and teachings.

TRADITIONAL DRAMA

Classical drama, known as *zat* (ZAHT), is very popular in Myanmar. The *zat* is based on the 550 Jataka tales told by the Buddha. In these tales the Buddha describes his previous existences and meetings with relatives, enemies, and disciples. The Buddha's heroic deeds, courage, and wisdom are portrayed prior to his achieving enlightenment.

The *zat* performance includes dancing and singing, and takes place in a *zat-yone*, a bamboo structure with a stage, or an open-air enclosure

Players put on an emotional *zat* performance.

with a bamboo matting fence. The *zat* usually starts late at night, and finishes at dawn. The audience sits on mats that they have bought for a few kyats per mat. The number of mats bought by a family group is governed by how many family members have come to watch the performance. They will bring food and snacks with them, and usually *lepet* (pickled tea), cheroots, and betel nut as well, to help ward off tiredness. It is quite common for some of the audience to doze during parts of the performance.

Yamazat is another well-known drama and is the Myanmar version of the Hindu epic *Ramayana*. The main characters are the princes Yama and Lekkhana, Princess Thida, Hanuman the monkey, and the ogre. The actors all wear masks.

THE MARIONETTE THEATER

Myanmar puppetry was well established during the Pagan era in the 11th century but has gone through phases of revival and decline. During the Kone Bong Era (1820—85) it was very popular partly because human dancers were not permitted on the stage but lifeless marionette dancers could be on a

Puppeteers with their marionettes.

high-level stage in front of the royal audience. The human manipulators of the puppets, and the singer, were hidden from view.

There are traditionally 28 puppets in the play, which depict the 28 *rupas* (physical forms) mentioned in the *Ah-bi-damma*, the Buddha's teachings. The themes of puppet plays are drawn from the 550 Jataka tales told by Buddha, and from historic Myanmar legends. The puppet sculptors observe strict rules regarding the choice of wood and materials they may use to make the particular figures, and the figures are accurate portrayals of the human anatomy. The puppets require great skill to manipulate, as some of them have as many as 60 strings and even their eyebrows move.

The Myanmar marionette theater was once a highly esteemed royal pastime, but with the demise of Myanmar the art experienced a sharp decline and now the marionette show is often is referred to as a dying art. However, in 1986, the Mandalay Marionettes Theatre was founded by two ladies, Ma Ma Naing and Naing Yee Mar, who had an interest in puppetry. They are building up a team of competent puppet players and musicians who perform in Myanmar and worldwide.

MODERN THEATER

The *pya-zat* is a relatively modern dance-drama that evolved from the Burmese court dance-drama *Zat Pwe*. The style of *pya-zat* is contemporary by comparison, emphasizes humor, and these days often includes songs to appeal to a wider audience. The *pya-zat* originated in the 1930s as a mime known as live bioscope, because it imitated silent movies but involved live actors. Unlike a Western musical, however, there is usually no dancing. The plays are performed on the stage and orchestras play below the stage. Speech is in prose, whereas traditional drama parts employ verse. Performances are set in the past and usually the princely hero overcomes wicked magicians and demons in a mysterious kingdom. These performances were hugely popular. Between 1943 and 1969 more than 200 plays were staged, of which approximately 180 were musical plays. Today these *pya-zat* are being revived and play to full houses.

DANCE

A Shan mask dancer performing the bird dance.

Myanmar dance has existed from pre-Buddhist times when *nat* (spirit) worship was performed with dance. Dance movements were strongly influenced by classical Indian and Thai dance. Myanmar dance is rather vigorous and requires some difficult acrobatic feats. It is also quite decorous; male and female dancers do not touch when they dance together. Young beginners are taught the *ka-bya-lut* (ker-biah-loot), a basic traditional dance. This dance is not accompanied by music but only with clappers and cymbals.

An interesting dance is one in which dancers perform like puppets. It has been said that Myanmar dance had to be copied from puppets because the marionette theater had replaced human dancers for a period. The principal female dancer wears a court dress with a bodice and long-sleeved jacket that has stiff curved edges at the hips; the *longyi* has a train that the dancer kicks out as she dances. Principal male dancers dress as princes in silk *longyi*, jacket, and white headdress. Other roles include pages, soldiers, *zawgyi* (zor-jee, meaning "wizard"), and nat.

The *yein* is a popular dance at the Water Festival celebrations to celebrate the new year. It involves uniformly dressed dancers, usually female, dancing in unison, The *hna-par-thwa* (ner-PAH-thwah) is a duet dance between a male and female. The elephant dance, performed at the Elephant Dance Festival in Kyaukse near Mandalay, has the dancers in a papier-mâché and bamboo-frame elephant costume.

The *anyeint* (er-nyayn) is a combination of solo dancing and clowning by *lu-pyet* (loo-pi-yairt), or clowns. The clowns sing, dance, compose impromptu speech, and make jokes about current events and various other topics, some of which are quite bawdy. During the intervals when the clowns appear, the dancer rests or changes her costume. Sometimes two or more dancers take turns dancing. The entire performance lasts about two hours.

Many of the ethnic dances are performed with swords or different kinds of drums. Ethnic dances include group dancing where young boys and girls dance together, which is not very common in Myanmar dance.

A traditional Myanmar orchestra is known as a *saing*.

MUSIC

Myanmar music can be disconcerting to the Western ear with its various separate sounds from drums, gongs, cymbals, bamboo clappers, flute, and Myanmar oboe. The sounds are in sharp contrast rather than in harmony.

When the Myanmar king Hsinbyushin Min invaded and conquered Siam (Thailand) in the 18th century, many Siamese musicians, dancers, composers, and craftspeople were brought to Myanmar. Myanmar culture and music has been greatly influenced by this augmentation. A type of classical song and dance is known as *yodaya*, meaning "Siamese." Western musical instruments such as the violin, piano, mandolin, guitar, and accordion have also been incorporated into Myanmar music over the decades.

The Myanmar orchestra, or *saing*, is dominated by percussion instruments and consists of a drum circle, gong circle, bamboo clappers, wind instruments including a *hne* (h-NAIR)—which has a high-pitched sound and is also called the Myanmar oboe—flute, and cymbals. Apart from the drum circle, there is also a large drum hung from an ornamental winged dragon.

The drum and gong circles are bright and colorful, decorated with glass mosaic and gold paint; they can be taken apart to be transported and reassembled at the performance location. There are 21 drums in a large drum circle, and nine in a small drum circle. A gong circle has 19 gongs. Sometimes, instead of a gong circle, there is a gong rectangle that consists of a row of gongs hung in a rectangular frame; this has fewer gongs than a gong circle.

Different kinds of drums are used for different celebrations. The *sidaw* (see-dor, or large drum) is for important formal occasions, the *ozi* (oh-zee, meaning "pot-shaped drum") and *dobat* (doh-baht, meaning "two-faced drum") are for village celebrations, and the *bonshay* (long drum) and *bongyi* (bohn-jee, meaning "big drum") are for plowing and harvesting festivals. A Myanmar drum is tuned with a piece of dough made of boiled rice and wood ash, which is stuck to the base of the drum to determine its tone. A melody can be played on the drum circle as the drums have different tones.

The *saung-gauk* (SAONG-goak) Myanmar harp is a 13-stringed instrument shaped like a boat. The harpist sits and holds the harp in the lap when playing. Classical songs are accompanied by the harp. The *pattalar* (PAHT-ter-LAH) xylophone is made of wooden or bamboo pieces.

There are many ethnic musical instruments and they vary in shape and material. The Chin have an oboe-like instrument, the *bu-hne* (boo-hnair), which is a gourd containing a number of bamboo reeds. The Mon gong circle is a curved horse-shoe shape lined with gongs. The Kayah have a bamboo flute with different lengths of bamboo attached to each other in a triangular shape.

LITERATURE

The earliest Myanmar literature was primarily of a religious nature and was inscribed on stone. These inscriptions go as far back as the Bagan period in the 11th century.

Palm-leaf manuscripts and folded paper manuscripts came into existence only after the 15th century. The literature during this period was mainly concerned with the Jataka tales told by the Buddha to his disciples in answer to certain questions. It was in the form of drama and epistles or missives, written in verse. Works on law and history were written in prose. Many dramas were written during the 16th to 18th centuries, while in the 19th century, poems, drama, and chronicles were produced.

After Myanmar fell to the British, the country's literature began to reflect the impact of Western culture; the arrival of the printing press also

MYAZEDI INSCRIPTION

The Myazedi inscription is a four-sided engraved stone executed in A.D. *1113 by Prince Rajakumara. It records the story of King Kyanzittha's deathbed reconciliation with his estranged son, whom he had disinherited. The epigraph is written in the Burmese, Pyu, Mon, and Pali languages and was discovered in 1887. The discovery of this inscription both proved that Burmese was used in the Bagan period and permitted the deciphering of the Pyu language, which had not been possible previously.*

influenced literature, which previously had been written for a much smaller audience. Plays that had been written for the court became widely available; these plays were not performed on the stage but were meant to be read.

Novels were a later development; the first Myanmar novel (1904) was an adaptation of Alexander Dumas's *The Count of Monte Cristo*, but written in a Myanmar setting.

Myanmar classical literature is flowery with long, difficult sentences and is concerned with the supernatural and magical. Originating from the court of the Myanmar kings, it was greatly influenced by Buddhist Pali and Sanskrit sources.

Modern Myanmar literature can be said to have had its beginnings in the 1930s when the University of Rangoon was founded and the Department of Myanmar Studies established. There was a new movement in literature known as the Khitsam movement whose writers used a simple and direct style that has continued to this day.

Present-day literature is still dominated by religious works, although there are many novels, short stories, poems, children's books, translations of foreign works, and works on culture, art, and science. Popular fiction consists mostly of romantic novels. Literary awards are presented annually. Many well-known writers are retired government servants, some of whom have worked or are working in institutes of higher learning. Most writers have a permanent job and write only in their spare time.

Men beating gold leaves, which are usually used by Buddhist devotees to place on the surface of pagodas.

CRAFTS

In Myanmar craftspeople and artisans are still able to make a living in spite of gradual industrialization. Among Myanmar's many traditional crafts are silk and cotton weaving, lacquerware, gold and silverwork, wood and ivory carving, mosaics, tapestry-making, stone carving, boat-making, umbrella-making, and pottery.

The cotton and silk *longyi* that Myanmar men and women still wear, despite the growing popularity of Western dress among the young, are handwoven. Rakhine is famous for cotton woven *longyi* in the beautiful *acheik* (er-chayk) design of twisted chains and spirals. Mandalay, Amarapura, and Pyi (or Pyay) are also famous for cotton woven fabrics, while Mudon, near Mawlamyine, is known for its cotton woven tablecloths and blankets. Fabric for silk *longyi* is woven in Mandalay and Amarapura and the Shan states. A favorite design is the beautiful multicolored *luntaya* (loon-ter-yah), or hundred shuttles. Other handwoven items include shawls and blankets from Pakokku in northwestern Myanmar and shoulder bags from Shan and Kachin, which are woven on a back-strap loom.

Tapestries, known as *kalagas* (ker-lah-gah), are popular tourist purchases and are made of appliqué designs on velvet or cotton cloth with glass beads and sequins stitched in. Traditional weaving designs include images of dancers, peacocks, elephants, and mythical animals.

Lacquerware is an ancient craft called *pan yun* (pan-yoon), it is one of the traditional arts and crafts metaphorically known as the Ten Flowers. Bagan and Pyi are lacquerware-producing areas. Typical articles are ashtrays, trinket boxes, vases, bowls, tables, and chests. The process involves coating a framework of woven bamboo with *thit-si* (raw lacquer obtained from a tree) and clay. The article is dried, after which several other coatings are applied. Finally, a design is hand-painted on the article.

Gold leaf is regularly placed on the surface of pagodas as a form of worship. The gold-leaf industry is located in Mandalay. Gold is pounded until it is very thin, placed between thick bamboo paper, and packed for sale at pagodas. Golden ornaments set with gems are worn by Myanmar women and treated as a form of investment. There are goldsmiths in every town, where women come to sell and buy jewelry or have old jewelry reset in modern designs.

Silverware was once very popular. Myanmar women wore silver belts, and silver bowls were used by the well-to-do for weddings and festivals. But these articles are slowly becoming rare as family heirlooms, as their owners sell them to supplement incomes.

Pottery-making in Myanmar consists of plain earthenware for cooking pots, flowerpots, and water pots, and glazed ware for water jars, flower vases, pickle jars, and various small glazed articles such as ashtrays.

A craft related to religion is the making of Buddha images. Marble Buddha images are carved in Mandalay, while those cast in brass, copper, or silver are made at Ywataung near Mandalay.

INTERNET LINKS

www.ancientbagan.com/bagan-lacquerware.htm

This site provides detailed information on the origins and process of producing lacquerware.

www.mandalaymarionettes.com/aboutus.html

This comprehensive site of contemporary marionette theater has information on the tradition of marionettes in Myanmar and includes links to the history of puppets and international performances.

www.myanmar.com/artsandliterature/index.html

This site has links to traditional arts and crafts, musical instruments, traditional dances, costumes, painting, and handicrafts.

LEISURE

A young monk about to go kite-flying.

11

Myanmar people have many different ways of enjoying their leisure time and importance is placed on family outings and social gatherings. For most non-urban Myanmar local entertainment involves sitting around with friends at home or in the local tea shop, telling jokes, and recounting the events of the day.

LEISURE TIME FOR THE MYANMAR tends to be in the evening when the adults have returned from work and children have completed their homework.

GAMES

One game, the *htoke-see-htoe* (TOHK-see-toh), is usually played on full-moon nights, and involves a lot of running and perspiration. Played with two teams, one team guards lines or rows that the other team tries to pass through.

Most Myanmar children have plenty of ingenuity and imagination: Old, flat sardine cans are turned into cars by tying a string and pulling

Children playing a board game.

Three rickshaw riders take a break and play a board game.

the can around, old bicycle tire rims are rolled along with a stick, and banana leaves and stems are made into toy guns, rings, and bracelets. Slingshots are easily made by carving a small piece of wood into a Y shape and tying a piece of rubber tubing to it. Pellets are made of mud from river banks, patiently rolled into small balls and dried in the sun.

Kites are flown in fields. The strings, rubbed with starch and glass powder, are so sharp that they can cut hands and even blind eyes. On a windy day kites are flown with the main purpose of bringing down another kite by cutting it adrift.

On the tamer side checkers can be played with bottle caps on cardboard boards. Grandparents teach their grandchildren to fold paper into ships, boats, animals, and other interesting objects. With so many kinds of games and playthings, there is almost no need for dolls and electronic toys.

SPORTS

Soccer is Myanmar's favorite and most popular sport. The spectators at national league soccer matches always fill the Thuwunna Youth Training

Children get muddy as they play one of Myanmar's most popular games, soccer, on a soggy field after the rain.

Center Stadium (or more commonly Thuwunna YTC Stadium). This 32,000-seat stadium, built in 1985, is smaller but more modern compared to the Aung San Stadium and is now the venue chosen by most national and international level football and track and field competitions. During the 1960s and 1970s Myanmar's national team was foremost in Southeast Asia, but in recent years it has declined in performance. Myanmar played its first-ever World Cup qualifiers in 2007, losing 0—7 and 0—4 to China. Soccer is played from boyhood with any kind of ball and is exciting to play and watch.

Chinlon is a traditional sport played with a woven rattan ball about 4.7 inches (12 cm) in diameter. The ball is hollow inside and about 16 inches (41 cm) in circumference. In formal games six players stand in a circle and try to keep the ball in the air using only their knees, heels, toes, elbows, shoulders, and head in a series of different techniques. They may not use their hands. It is a simple game but requires great skill and good teamwork in tossing the ball around. The game may also be played informally, with

A group of young people playing *chinlon* on one of Myanmar's alleyways.

a single person or any number of players, and the main objective is to keep the ball airborne. *Chinlon* was once played to entertain the king, but it declined in popularity during the colonial period. In post-independence times there have been great efforts to revive and promote it, and many *chinlon* associations have been formed. There are even women players who are so skilled that they can keep several cane balls going at once. A variation of *chinlon* is played like volleyball, over a net, with two teams participating, but they still do not use their hands.

Myanmar boxing is very violent even to most Myanmar spectators. The boxers are allowed to use any part of the body to fight. A number of rules, such as no kicking in the groin, no scratching, no biting, and no hair pulling, have to be observed. A boxer who is down may not be hit or kicked in any way. If a contestant cannot rise after the count of eight, or goes down three times, a knockout is declared. The match may be won by the person who draws first blood, which is actually fourth blood, as each boxer is allowed to wipe blood away three times before being declared the loser. The boxer's

Myanmar boxers at training.

class is not determined by body weight, but by skill. A youngster begins in the lowest fourth class and moves up when he gets too good for his opponents in the same class. In more formal matches, fighters are matched by weight and build within their own class. However, when a boxer reaches first class, he has to take on all opponents. Boxing matches, featuring famous boxers, travel from town to town and can be found at pagoda festivals. Boxing matches are accompanied by a Myanmar orchestra. Matches usually take place after the harvest until just before the rainy season.

Thaing is a Myanmar traditional martial art and a form of self-defense that originated over 2,000 years ago during the reign of King Okkalapa when it was officially practiced among warriors of the royal army. It declined during colonial years but was revived in 1958 by patriotic professionals who established the Myanmar Thaing Institute in Yangon. In recent years it has been popularized in movies, comic strips, and novels featuring the heroes from the days of the kings.

In the villages cockfighting is still found. It is a cruel sport because spurs are sharpened so as to hurt or kill the opponent. The spectators place bets.

Western sports such as tennis, golf, volleyball, basketball, and badminton are played in urban areas, but some sports such as cricket and baseball are not widely known. Rowing, yachting, table tennis, cycling, and hiking are also sports that have a number of enthusiasts in Yangon. Myanmar's track and field record in Southeast Asia has been outstanding, especially in the marathon.

STORYTELLING

Storytelling is common in the upbringing of children by all ethnic and social groups in Myanmar. Stories are told by grandparents, aunts, older sisters, and cousins to younger children to keep them quiet and to teach them good morals such as honesty, diligence, generosity, and faith. Most children love stories, and the favorite storyteller aunts and cousins on a visit may be pestered until they give in and tell a story or two. There are many kinds of stories—folktales; ethnic tales; humorous tales; tales of kings, queens, princes, and princesses; and most important of all, the Jataka tales and the Dhamma-pada—tales from the Buddha's life.

Folktales are handed down by word of mouth from generation to generation, and they tell of Master Golden Rabbit, Master Tiger, Master Fox, and some other animals' adventures that are funny and full of lessons to be learned. Master Simpleton, Mr. and Mrs. Deaf, and Mr. Clever are some of the typical characters of folktales.

Ethnic tales are told to preserve ethnic legends about the origin of the people of each group, their customs, and the meaning of the various festivals or celebrations. Humorous tales, some of which would not be mentioned in other societies, are accepted as natural and worthy of a hearty laugh. Tales of kings and life at court tell of heroes famous for qualities such as strength, courage, and perseverance in the face of danger and seemingly hopeless situations.

THE RABBIT'S COLD

Once upon a time a lion lived in a cave. His loyal subjects were the bear, the monkey, and the rabbit. One day the lion came up with an idea to obtain food easily. First of all he called the bear to him, opened his mouth wide, and asked him what kind of smell he could smell. The bear said, "Oh, Lion, I smell the smell of rotten meat." "What!" said the lion. "How dare you say that to me, the King of the Forest?" He bit the bear and ate him up.

Next he turned to the monkey and asked him the same question. Having seen what had happened to the honest bear, the monkey said, "Oh, Lion, your mouth has the fragrance of lilies." "What!" said the lion. "I who live on the meat of lesser animals cannot possibly have such fragrance issuing from my mouth! Do you dare to lie to me?" So the monkey went the same way as the bear.

Last was the rabbit's turn. The rabbit did not come up close to the lion, but said, "Oh, Lion, I have such a very bad cold, and my nose cannot detect any smell whatsoever. Allow me to go home and cure my cold first, please." With that the rabbit ran away as fast as he could and never went near the lion's cave again.

INTERNET LINKS

www.myanmars.net/myanmar-culture/myanmar-games.htm

This website illustrates traditional and popular Myanmar games.

www.myanmarfootball.org/

This is the official website of the Myanmar Football (soccer) Federation.

www.seasite.niu.edu/burmese/

This site (by the Center of Southeast Asian Studies, North Illinois University) details the language, literature, and culture of Myanmar.

FESTIVALS

Participants of the traditional annual Kachin Manau festival.

12

The traditional Myanmar calendar is a lunisolar calendar based on both the phases of the sun and the phases of the moon. It consists of 12 lunar months and within each month of the Myanmar calendar a major festival is held, usually Myanmar Buddhist.

THE MYANMAR CALENDAR features 12 lunar months of 28 days each that run out of sync with the months of the solar Gregorian calendar. In order to synchronize with the rest of the world, the country adds a second Waso (June/July) lunar month every four years. Pyatho 1368 corresponds to January 2007.

For religious matters the Myanmar use the Buddhist calendar, which is also the lunar calendar, but the calculation begins from the year of the

A dragon dance troupe performing as part of Chinese New Year celebrations.

THE MYANMAR CALENDAR

Myanmar months and corresponding English months:

Tagu	*mid-March to mid-April*
Kason	*mid-April to mid-May*
Nayon	*mid-May to mid-June*
Waso	*mid-June to mid-July*
Wagaung	*mid-July to mid-August*
Tawthalin	*mid-August to mid-September*
Thadingyut	*mid-September to mid-October*
Tazaungmon	*mid-October to mid-November*
Nadaw	*mid-November to mid-December*
Pyatho	*mid-December to mid-January*
Tabodwe	*mid-January to mid-February*
Tabaung	*mid-February to mid-March*

Buddha's Enlightenment: 2000 was the year 2543—2544 on the Buddhist calendar. Local festival dates are not fixed as they normally take place or culminate on days of the full moon.

WATER FESTIVAL

There is a festival for each month of the Myanmar calendar, beginning with the first month of Tagu.

In mid-April, to welcome the New Year, the Water Festival is celebrated. Over a four- to five-day period water is thrown around and everyone gets a thorough soaking. Anyone is fair game for a drenching, except for monks and pregnant women. Symbolically the water washes away the previous year's sins and bad luck, and the mind and spirit are purified in readiness for welcoming the New Year. This festival occurs at the hottest time of the year when the temperature may reach 104°F (40°C) so the water soaking can actually be welcome, and it does not take too long to dry in the heat anyway!

Crowds being sprayed with water during the Water Festival in Mandalay.

At the side of the road special temporary bamboo structures called *mandats* (MUN-DART) are erected. In front of these open-sided shelters, water barrels and even high-powered water jets are set up and the occupants of the shelter proceed to drench anyone and everything that passes by. The Myanmar tour around the city in open-sided jeeps with the apparent intention of getting as wet as possible, even lining up in front of the *mandats* awaiting their turn for a soaking. The event is accompanied by loud music and dancing and the general mood is for everyone to have a good time.

On the final day of the festival the Theravada Buddhist religious traditions of setting free fish, birds, and cattle are followed. The elderly have their hair washed by the youngsters who thereby gain merit, and special feasts are given to the monks in the monasteries.

On April 15, 2010, a series of bomb explosions, purportedly set by ethnic rebels or exile groups, during the Water Festival killed nine people and injured 170 in Yangon.

BANYAN TREE-WATERING CEREMONY

The banyan, sacred fig, or bo tree (*Ficus religiosa*) is believed to be the tree under which the Buddha attained enlightenment. Banyan trees in Myanmar are revered by Buddhists. The month of Kason is at the height of the dry season, so the earth is parched. Water is poured on the trees to ensure they do not die in case of drought. During the festival, Kason Buddhist devotees process to the banyan tree to celebrate the water pouring ceremony and also to perform meritorious deeds by offering flowers, light, water, and incense to the images of the Buddha.

WASO ROBE-OFFERING CEREMONY (DHAMMA-SET-KYA DAY)

The Myanmar month of Waso corresponds to the Gregorian calendar month of July, and it is one of the holiest months of all in the Myanmar Buddhist calendar. Four Great Happenings of Lord Gautama Buddha are believed to have occurred during the full-moon day of Waso. Lord Buddha was conceived; he renounced all his worldly attachments to seek Nirvana (when he was still a prince); he preached his first sermon, and he showed his omniscient powers to a group of heretics. The full-moon day of Waso also marks the beginning of the Buddhist Lent, a three-month period that lasts until October. Monks are confined to their monasteries in this period, but they still need to go about their daily rounds for alms. As they need a change of robes, lay persons are permitted to offer the monks Waso Thingan or Waso Holy Robes. Devotees gather at the monasteries, listen to sermons, observe the 10 Holy Commandments, and offer the new robes to the monks. The 10 Holy Commandments of Buddhism are as follows: Do not destroy life; do not take what is not given you; do not commit adultery; tell no lies and deceive no one; do not become intoxicated; eat temperately and not at all in the afternoons; do not watch dancing, nor listen to singing or plays; wear no garlands, perfumes or any adornments; sleep not in luxurious beds; accept no gold or silver.

Devotees at Shwedagon Pagoda to observe Tazaungmon, a Buddhist festival that celebrates the full moon.

FESTIVAL OF LIGHTS

The Festival of Lights is celebrated at the end of Lent on the full-moon day of Thadingyut, which coincides with the end of the rainy season. This festival commemorates the descent of the Buddha to Earth at the end of the three months of Lent when he preached to his divine mother the Buddhist Abidhamma, the most difficult of Buddhist teachings. Buddhist homes are lit up at night with paper lanterns hung on front porches or candles. Government offices and buildings are decorated with colorful electric lights. The festival lasts three days, from the eve of the full moon to the day after the full moon.

Since this festival marks the end of Lent, it is a time of great joy. Some streets are closed off at night and stages are erected at one end for all-night performances by dancers, comedians, singers, and musicians. Small stalls are set up, selling local foods and handicrafts.

A boy prepares himself for festivities of his *shin pyu*, the initiation of his novicehood as a monk.

It is the custom for young people to show their respect and gratitude to parents, teachers, and mentors by going to their homes with gifts of cakes, fruits, and other offerings. In making these offerings, the young people sit on the floor and make the gesture of obeisance three times, while the elders give blessings for good health, wealth, and safe passage through life.

KAHTEIN ROBE-OFFERING CEREMONY

The Kahtein robe-offering ceremony is performed during the month of Tazaungmone (mid-October to mid-November). Robes and other articles are offered to monks; feasts are also held, with many guests invited to take part in the merit-making.

A second festival of lights is held at this time, a month after the first festival of lights; again it lasts three days, from the eve of the full-moon day to the day after the full moon.

At Yangon's Shwe Dagon pagoda, an all-night weaving contest takes place where weavers spend the night weaving robes that must be completed at dawn when they are offered to the Buddha images at the pagoda. Other such all-night weaving takes place around the country.

On the night of the full moon, there is a custom of hiding other people's possessions in various places as a joke; for example, people might move the neighbors' flowerpots or water barrels, or remove the clothesline.

HTA-MA-NE MAKING FESTIVAL

This festival celebrates the harvest and takes place in the month of Ta-bo-dwei. *Hta-ma-ne* (ter-mah-NAIR) is made from glutinous rice, peanuts, ginger, oil, garlic, sesame seeds, and coconut. The ginger, garlic, and coconut are sliced thinly and added to the glutinous rice, and the mixture is cooked in large pans over open fires on monastery grounds or in private gardens. The mixture is so sticky that it has to be stirred by grown men with big wooden paddles. This rich and fragrant pudding is served to everyone.

Celebrations at festivals often include Ferris wheels.

PAGODA FESTIVALS

Myanmar is a land of pagodas, and the more famous pagodas have their own festival days. The Shwe Dagon Pagoda festival is held around the full-moon day of Tabaung, the last month of the year.

Pagoda festivals have Ferris wheels, all-night shows and dances, and stalls that sell food, local handicrafts, and souvenirs. Villagers from all around attend, spending the night watching shows, eating favorite delicacies, and going home in their bullock carts in the morning.

ETHNIC FESTIVALS

Each of the ethnic groups in Myanmar has its own festivals. Of these the better known ones are the Kayin New Year, the Kachin Manao festival, and the Pa-o rocket-firing festivals.

KAYIN NEW YEAR is celebrated on the new-moon day of the lunar month, Pya-tho, and is a national holiday. In Yangon, Karens gather at communal centers, and Don dances are performed by Karen girls and boys wearing the

HPAUNG-DAW-U FESTIVAL

In the month of Tawthalin, a unique pagoda festival, the Hpaung-Daw-U festival, takes place in Inle Lake in eastern Myanmar. Here, on and around Inle Lake, the Inthas live, weaving silk and cotton, fishing, and growing vegetables on floating gardens. They travel around in boats either rowed with oars or powered by outboard motors. The rowing is done in a standing position with one leg wrapped around the oar; hence, the Inthas are known as the "leg rowers of Inle Lake."

During this festival three Buddha images from the pagoda are taken around on the lake in lovely decorated boats so that the people can worship from their own boats and homes as the images pass.

Karen dress. In Pa-an, capital of the Karen State, the Don is performed with great ceremony. Frog drums and buffalo horns are played.

KACHIN MANAO FESTIVAL The Kachins celebrate a victory or a prosperous period, or mark the illness or death of parents or the moving away of a family member with a Manao (mer-NOW) festival.

The Manao involves great expense since there are many guests. Only chieftains (*duwa*) are capable of bearing the expense; one such festival involved the slaughtering of 14 buffaloes, 20 cows, 20 pigs, and 50 chickens, and 200 baskets of rice and 4,500 bottles of spirits. A large shelter, decorated with a huge pair of buffalo horns, is built with four Manao poles in the center; drinking, eating, and dancing take place here.

PA-O ROCKET FESTIVAL This festival is celebrated by the Pa-o people who live in southern Shan State. During this festival lengths of large bamboo poles or metal shells are filled with gunpowder, fuses are attached, and the "rockets" are fired from a 20- to 30-foot-high (6- to 9-m-high) rocket stand. This festival is celebrated from Tagu to Waso, the first four months of the Myanmar year, as an offering to the gods for a favorable climate, good harvest, and prosperous and peaceful new year.

INTERNET LINKS

www.allmyanmar.com

This website provides general information on Myanmar, including details of annual festivals.

http://asiarecipe.com/burfestival.html

This site details monthly festivals in Myanmar, their dates, and locations.

www.travel-myanmar.net/festivals2010.htm

This site gives detailed information on festivals throughout the year.

FOOD

A woman selling produce at a market in Myitkyina.

13

MYANMAR FOOD IS NOT AS WELL known as the other Asian cuisines of Thailand, China, India, or Japan.

Myanmar people enjoy rice as their main food and it makes up about 75 percent of the diet. Rice is served with different kinds of stewed dishes and curries. Side dishes include salads and stir-fried or boiled vegetables with delicious spicy dips.

Myanmar has a saying "food is medicine, medicine is food." Many herbs and spices are used in Myanmar cooking not only to enhance the taste of a dish, but also for their medicinal properties.

KITCHENS

Myanmar kitchens are presided over by the female members of the household—the mother, elder daughters, aunts, or grandmothers.

In the kitchen a low round table about 1.5 feet (46 cm) in height is used, with low stools as seats. Common kitchen articles include a stone mortar and pestle, a chopping block—usually made of a round cross-section of a tree trunk—earthen or aluminum pots without handles, and earthen water jars. Wood or charcoal fires are used, since electricity and gas is available only in larger urban areas and kerosene is scarce.

Most of the kitchen activity takes place at floor level. Because the fresh meat and vegetables are bought without benefit of storage or packaging, a lot of cleaning has to be done immediately after their purchase. For this, and for the cleaning of large pots, a corner of

***Right*: An Intha woman making rice snacks.**

the kitchen usually has a water tap and water jars. Sometimes washing is done outside the kitchen in the backyard where water is stored in large barrels of wood or metal.

Myanmar households use a "cat" safe, *kyaung-ein* (chaung-ain), to store cooked foods, leftovers, plates, forks and spoons, spices, and ingredients in bottles. The safe is a small wooden cupboard about 4 to 5 feet (122 to 152 cm) in height, a foot (30.5 cm) in depth, and 2 feet (61 cm) wide. The sides and front are made of wire mesh to give proper airing for the food inside; a couple of drawers provide space for cutlery.

Rice is a staple at most Myanmar meals.

MAIN INGREDIENTS

Rice is included in all meals and most snacks. It can be eaten as a salad, fried, cooked with coconut cream, or kneaded with fish. Rice is usually served with mild curries made with vegetables, chicken, fish, or seafood. Glutinous rice is steamed, boiled, or rolled in banana leaves with banana stuffing. Rice flour is used in many dishes, cakes, and desserts.

The Myanmar use many spices and herbs in their cooking, including fresh ones. Turmeric, chili, onions, garlic, and ginger are pounded in a stone mortar and cooked in oil before meat, fish, or vegetables are added. Coriander leaf, lemon grass, tamarind juice, fish sauce, and fish paste are used in many dishes.

Myanmar women cook without the help of written recipes. Recipes are handed down through generations by word of mouth, and one learns by doing rather than reading. However, Myanmar cookbooks have gained popularity in the last decade.

The Myanmar also eat Western bread, cakes, and cookies, but wheat flour and other baking ingredients are scarce, and Western cakes are only for special occasions. People give cakes to parents and elders on festival days as a sign of respect.

A wide variety of fruits and vegetables are available in Myanmar, thanks to its diverse climate.

MEAT, VEGETABLES, AND FRUIT All kinds of meat are eaten by the Myanmar, but most people prefer fish, fish products, and shrimp. If meat is avoided it is usually beef because the cow, used to plow the soil for rice, is regarded as a benefactor. Buddhists believe slaughtering a large animal for its meat is more sinful than killing a smaller one. Certain meats cannot be offered as food to monks, including bear, elephant, snake, and tiger meat. Some monks are vegetarian, although there is no specific religious taboo on meat. Many laypeople avoid meat during the Buddhist Lenten months from July to October.

The Myanmar like to eat raw or blanched vegetables with fish sauce dips and to drink soups made from the freshly plucked tender leaves of certain tropical trees and shrubs. They enjoy eating the roselle (*Hibiscus sabdariffa*) leaf, a sour-tasting vegetable, and water greens, also known as the aquatic morning glory (*Ipomea aquatica*). Okra (*Abelmoschus esculentus*), drumstick-fruit (*Moringa oleifera*, a vegetable), gourd (a large green fruit of the gourd vine), chayote (*Sechium edule*), and eggplant are common vegetables. Backyard gardens provide fresh vegetables, and trees, in abundance even in and around the cities, provide fruit and tender leaves.

Because of the varied climate in the different regions of Myanmar, a wide variety of tropical and temperate vegetables and fruits is available. Many Myanmar plant their own vegetables and fruits.

Fruits such as strawberries, avocados, and oranges were introduced during the colonial period, while grapefruit and apples were introduced as late as the 1950s. Common local fruits are mango, durian, mangosteen,

BETEL BOX (*KOON-IT*)

Betel-chewing is quite common among the Myanmar, and it is customary to offer monks betel for chewing in a lacquer betel box. Betel boxes come in tiers that have special small compartments in each tier for the required ingredients: betel leaves, betel nuts, white lime, and spices, and a metal betel-nut cutter.

Lacquer betel boxes come in many designs: red and green, gold and black, and an embossed gold and black design that is now very rare.

rambutan, tangerine, pear, watermelon, and jackfruit. Myanmar like to eat fruit peeled and cut to savor the taste of each individual piece.

TRADITIONAL MYANMAR FARE

Since Myanmar lies between India and China, both Indian and Chinese influences can be found in the cuisine. Many Myanmar dishes are cooked in a Chinese manner, including stir-frying and using typical Chinese ingredients such as bean curd, bean sprouts, and soy sauce. Indian influence can be seen in the use of spices for curries. On special occasions Myanmar serve biryani, an Indian dish of chicken cooked with spices and served with saffron rice.

A traditional Myanmar main meal consists of boiled rice, a soup, a salad, a curry of meat or fish, and vegetables eaten raw with fish-paste sauce, boiled, or fried. In rural areas, meat curries are only an occasional treat.

For breakfast most Myanmar like to eat *mohinga* (mo-hin-gah), rice noodles in a fish soup. Certain towns in Myanmar are famous for different types of *mohinga*. Steamed glutinous rice with toasted dried fish, sesame powder, and grated coconut is also a favorite. Another breakfast favorite is *nan-piah* (nan-PIAH), a flat Indian wheat bread, eaten with boiled beans tossed in oil and salt dressing. Fried rice made from leftover rice from the previous evening also makes an adequate breakfast. Bread is eaten only in the main urban areas, and even then, only occasionally.

SNACKS, SALADS, AND DESSERTS

Traditional sweet cakes.

Many Myanmar enjoy eating fried snacks, which are usually fritters of onions, beans, bananas, or gourd. Myanmar salads are made of raw or boiled vegetables, or meat mixed with sliced onion, garlic, dried shrimp powder, ground peanuts, roasted bean powder, fish sauce, lime or tamarind juice, and oil (which is cooked with turmeric to remove the oily taste).

Dessert may be fruit, peeled and cut to retain its natural taste, fruit preserves, nuts, or *jaggery* (palm sugar balls) served with plain tea. Traditional desserts are made from coconut, rice, or glutinous rice flour, and jaggery. Coconut cream is an essential ingredient in traditional Myanmar desserts. Many desserts have fancy names such as "golden heart cooler," "butterfly," and "smooth as marble."

DRINKS

Alcohol is avoided by most Myanmar who are devout Buddhists, except perhaps for rare social occasions and in the urban areas. The drinking of alcohol in any form is generally regarded as an indication of poor morals and constitutes a violation of basic Buddhist precepts. However, a traditional wine made from toddy palm or *dani* (der-NI) (a palm that grows in swamps) is drunk by those in rural areas as a pastime or at festivals.

The only drink at the end of a meal is water or Myanmar tea. Coffee or tea is drunk at breakfast or sometimes at tea time, in a ready-mix brew with condensed milk. Soft drinks, known as aerated water in Myanmar, are served on special occasions.

Two men enjoy a cup of tea in the evening.

Alcoholic drinks are sold freely in Myanmar. However, the Myanmar people mostly practice temperance, and there are no drinking customs as such among the Myanmar. Social drinking is mostly found among Western-educated Myanmar. Generally drinking is associated with alcoholism.

Ethnic Burmans drink toddy wine or *dani* wine, while most of the other ethnic groups drink wine made from rice or glutinous rice. A low-quality home brew called country spirits, or "CS," is made from rice or corn and is available all over the country.

Among the ethnic groups, the Chin people who live in the western mountains drink a sweet wine, *khaung yei* (kaong-yay). They have the custom of drinking wine with a friend from the same container, usually a bamboo section. *Hlaw sa* (hlor-zah), the fermented rice from which *khaung yei* is extracted, can be eaten as a kind of pudding.

Many ethnic groups celebrate festivities with drinking. At the Kachin Manao Festival, it is said that up to 3,000 bottles of *khaung yei* and 1,500 bottles of country spirits are needed for the numerous guests. The Pa-O people living in the Shan State also drink in celebration before the rocket-firing festival. Ethnic Karens drink at funerals and at bone-collecting ceremonies.

MEALTIMES

Mealtimes in Myanmar are generally earlier than Western mealtimes. In rural areas, the family wakes before dawn, at about 4:00 A.M., and breakfast is at about 5:00 or 6:00 A.M. In the urban areas breakfast is at about 7:00 A.M. The

ROADSIDE WATER-POT STAND

The gift of water holds special significance for Buddhists who believe it brings 10 merits: longevity, beauty, riches, strength, knowledge, cleanliness, fame, friends, never being in need of water, and being as swift as flowing water.

Buddhists offer water to the Buddha in household shrines, dig wells, and build water-pot stands for thirsty travelers in order to gain religious merit. These small stands are four-legged and made of wood, with a roof to give cover to the pots and cups. The base around the pot is sometimes filled with sand to keep the water cool, and bright green rice seedlings are grown in the sand to lighten the heart of the weary.

midday meal is eaten at about noon; office workers carry their own food to the office in a small lunch box or tiered lunch carrier. In place of afternoon tea, a main meal is served at about 5:00 P.M. In urban areas where there is little or no night life, a light snack with a pot of Myanmar tea might be sufficient for supper at 10:00 or 11:00 P.M. Bedtime is even earlier in villages due to the lack of electricity and other lighting fuel.

TABLE MANNERS

The Myanmar do not dine in the Western sense of savoring food or wines and making conversation. The meal is quickly eaten and is over when one is full. There is no lingering at the dinner table, and guests may leave quite soon after eating. Dishes are full of flavor, but there is no emphasis on decoration or garnish. A meal does not consist of different courses. Instead, the dishes are placed in the center of the kitchen table, usually a low round table, with the diners seated on low stools as seats. In urban houses, there are Western-type dining tables and chairs. There is no specific seating arrangement. Portions from all the dishes are placed on one's plate and eaten with rice.

The most important eating etiquette is to serve the head of the family or oldest member first. Even if this person is not present at the time, it is customary to reserve the first portion for him or her. Many Myanmar feel that eating with fingers is more conducive to hearty enjoyment of the meal. The hands must be washed first. Only the right hand is used and polite manners dictate that food must never touch the area beyond the first digits.

Generally there is not much conversation during the meal. Talking with one's mouth full, talking about topics such as body wastes, and making noises are all considered inappropriate and must be avoided at all costs. Eating too slowly, lying down or slouching, and sighing are regarded as being disrespectful at the meal table.

If there are guests, they should be pressed to have some more food, and even if they say no, their host may insist on serving them another portion. This is part of the Myanmar hospitality.

A young boy cheerily has his meal. The Myanmar believe that eating with one's fingers makes a meal more enjoyable.

FEASTS

A Myanmar feast usually involves an offering of food and other items to monks, with guests arriving later to join in. Such feasts may take place in one's own home or at a monastery. The number of guests varies from a few close relatives to hundreds arriving at staggered intervals throughout the day. The occasion for a feast may be a birthday, a novitiation (a period of training that a religious novice goes through before being called to a religious life), an ear-piercing ceremony, a christening, or a wedding anniversary. It could be to gain merit for one's deceased parents or for oneself by donating toward building a new monastery, or offering robes on festival days.

The most sumptuous dishes are served at these feasts. The wealthier the host, the greater the variety of dishes served. Pork, chicken, seafood, hilsa (a kind of fish), and butterfish are made into curries, and it is important that they be cooked to perfection. Many side dishes of salads and delicious desserts are also served.

If the feast is held in the home, close relatives may sometimes bring their offerings of food for the monks. The night before the feast is one of great activity. The living room has to be cleared of chairs and tables, and carpets or smooth mats laid out. Special places are set aside for the monks. If the food to be offered is cooked at home, a small army of cooks composed of relatives—with a repertoire of tasty dishes—and a number of volunteer helpers may be seen peeling and cleaning the onions, garlic, and ginger. The food to be cooked will have been bought on several marketing trips days before. The food is cooked during the night; the pots are so big that a fire using firewood has to be built outside in the backyard. In the villages all the villagers or neighbors may come to help or at least give support by their presence. If the feast is held in a monastery, it is customary to order the food or have it cooked on the grounds by staff from the monastery.

When the monks arrive, they are offered the food, after which a suitable sermon is delivered and certain sutras chanted to bestow on the audience protection from danger, illness, and misfortune. Then the host and hostess share their merit with all beings, and guests praise the merit by saying *sadhu* (sah-DOO, meaning "well-done") three times. Then the guests are served food.

INTERNET LINKS

www.myanmars.net/myanmar-food/

This site describes Myanmar food and includes many traditional recipes.

www.tuninst.net/MyanMedPlants/indx-DB.htm#Top

This is an online Myanmar medicinal plant database.

http://sstmyanmar.com/drupal/products-myanmar-toddy-palm

This site tells all about the uses of the toddy palm.

BURMESE PRAWN CURRY

1 cup (250 ml) oil

1 teaspoon (5 ml) turmeric

½ teaspoon (2.5 ml) chili powder

1 cup (250 ml) onion, sliced or pounded

1 clove garlic, sliced or pounded

1 or 2 tomatoes, diced

10 to 12 prawns, shelled and deveined

1 tablespoon (15 ml) fish sauce

1 or 2 sprigs of coriander, cut finely

Heat oil, and put in turmeric, chili powder, onion, and garlic. Fry until fragrant and dry. Add tomatoes and continue frying until tomatoes are soft. Add prawns and cook until the prawns turn pink. Slowly add the fish sauce over the prawns and stir lightly. Sprinkle the coriander over the prawns, and turn off the stove when the coriander is lightly cooked but still green. Serve with white rice and a green salad.

HTAMANE

1 cup (250 ml) vegetable oil

1 small piece of fresh ginger, cut into thin strips

1 cup (250 ml) glutinous rice (wash and soak in water overnight)

1 cup (250 ml) coconut milk, mixed with 1 teaspoon (5 ml) sugar

Water enough to come up to 0.79 inch (2 cm) above the rice (in the pan)

1 cup (250 ml) peanuts, roasted and skinned

1 cup (250 ml) sesame seeds, roasted

1 cup (250 ml) cashew nuts, roasted and lightly crushed (optional)

1 cup (250 ml) pistachio nuts, roasted and lightly crushed (optional)

3 cloves garlic, thinly sliced

1½ teaspoon (7.5 ml) salt

Hot water

Using a medium-sized wok, put in oil and heat until hot. Add ginger strips and fry until fragrant and light brown. Add glutinous rice and stir until well-coated with ginger oil. Next put in the water and coconut milk and stir until mixed. Cover and cook over low heat until the rice is cooked and very soft; add hot water, a little at a time, and keep stirring until the rice grains become mushy. Add peanuts, sesame seeds, cashew nuts, and pistachios, and continue stirring until well blended. Sprinkle salt and stir. *Htamane* is done when the oil is on top and all the water is absorbed. The mixture must be sticky and mushy.

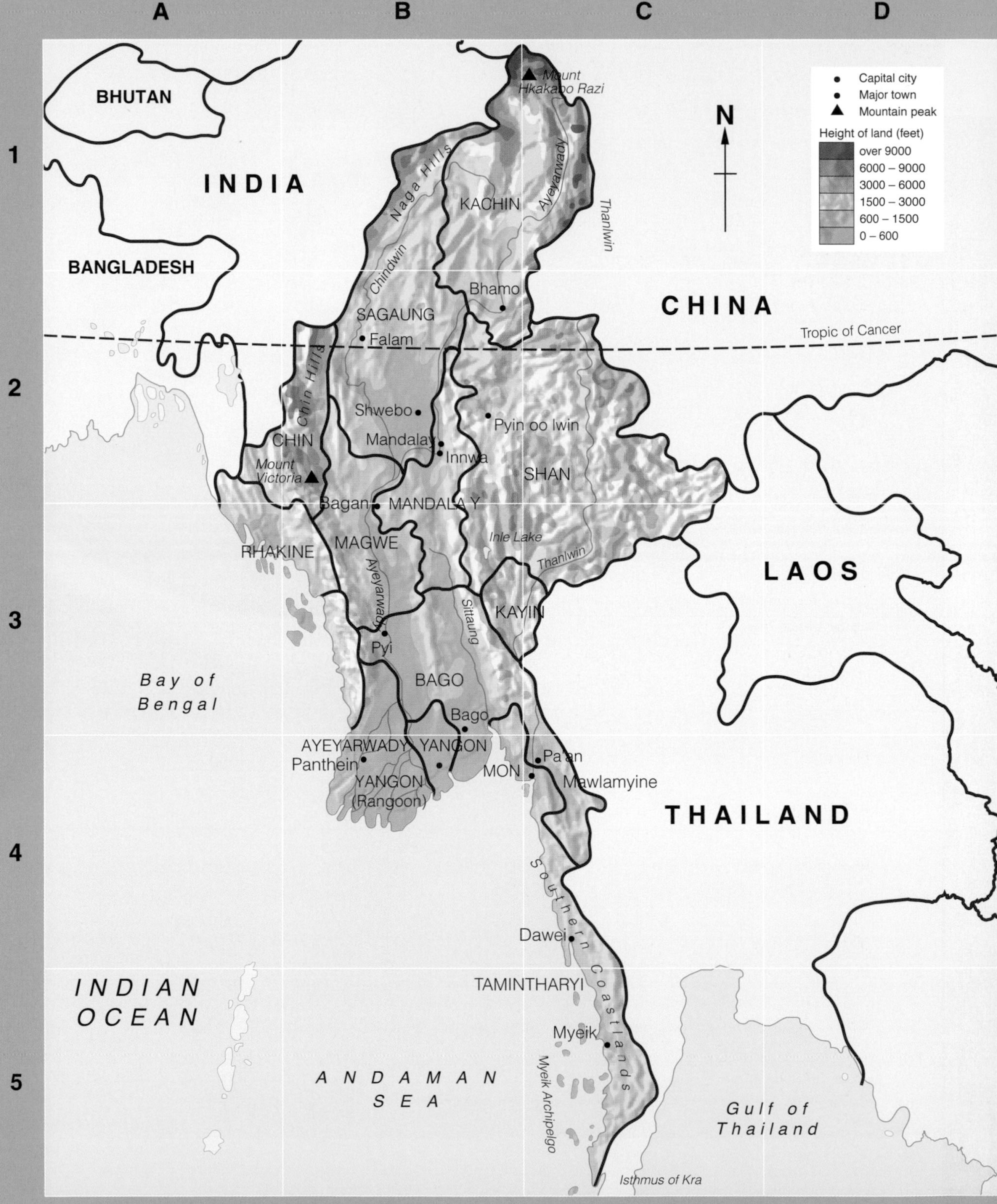

A
B
C
D
1
2
3
4
5
BHUTAN
INDIA
BANGLADESH
CHINA
LAOS
THAILAND
Mount Hkakabo Razi
Naga Hills
KACHIN
Ayeyarwady
Thanlwin
Chindwin
Bhamo
SAGAUNG
Falam
Tropic of Cancer
Chin Hills
Shwebo
Pyin oo lwin
Mandalay
Innwa
CHIN
Mount Victoria
SHAN
Bagan
MANDALAY
Inle Lake
RHAKINE
MAGWE
Thanlwin
Ayeyarwady
Sittaung
KAYIN
Pyi
Bay of Bengal
BAGO
Bago
AYEYARWADY
YANGON
Pa'an
Panthein
MON
Mawlamyine
YANGON (Rangoon)
Southern Coastlands
Dawei
INDIAN OCEAN
TAMINTHARYI
Myeik
Myeik Archipelgo
ANDAMAN SEA
Gulf of Thailand
Isthmus of Kra
N
Capital city
Major town
Mountain peak
Height of land (feet)
over 9000
6000 – 9000
3000 – 6000
1500 – 3000
600 – 1500
0 – 600

MAP OF MYANMAR

Andaman Sea, B5
Ayeyarwady (state), B4
Ayeyarwady River, C1—C3

Bagan, B2
Bago (state), B3
Bago (town), B3
Bangladesh, A1
Bengal, Bay of, A3
Bhamo, B2
Bhutan, A1

Chin, A2—B2
Chin Hills, B2
China, C1—D1
Chindwin River, B1, B2

Dawei, C4

Falam, B2

Gulf of Thailand, C5—D5

India, A1—B1
Indian Ocean, A4—A5
Inle Lake, B3—C3
Innwa, B2
Isthmus of Kra, B5, C5

Kachin, B1
Kayin (Karen), B3—C3

Laos, C3—D3

Magwe, B3
Mandalay (state), B2—B3
Mandalay (town), B2
Mawlamyine, C4
Mon, C4
Mount Hkakabo Razi, B1
Mount Victoria, B2
Myeik, C5
Myeik Archipelago, C5

Naga Hills, B1

Pa'an, C4
Pathein, B3
Pegu (state), B3
Pegu (town), B3
Pyi, B3
Pyin oo lwin (Maymyo), B2

Rakhine, A3—B3

Sagaung, B2
Shan, C2
Shwebo, B2
Sittaung River, B3
Southern coastlands, C4—C5

Tanintharyi, C4
Thailand, C4—D4
Thanlwin River, C1—C3

Yangon (state), B3
Yangon (town), B3

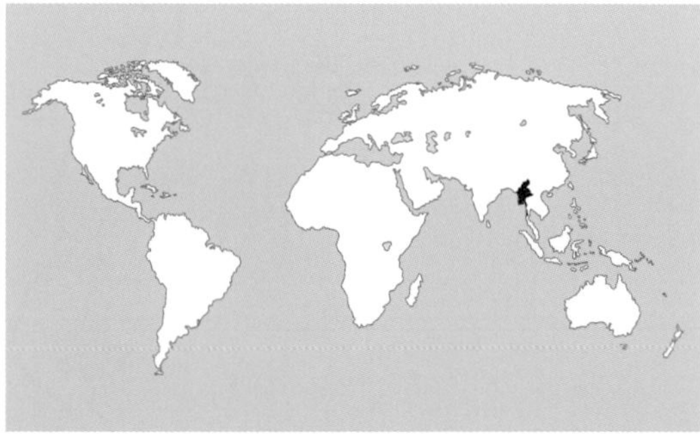

ECONOMIC MYANMAR

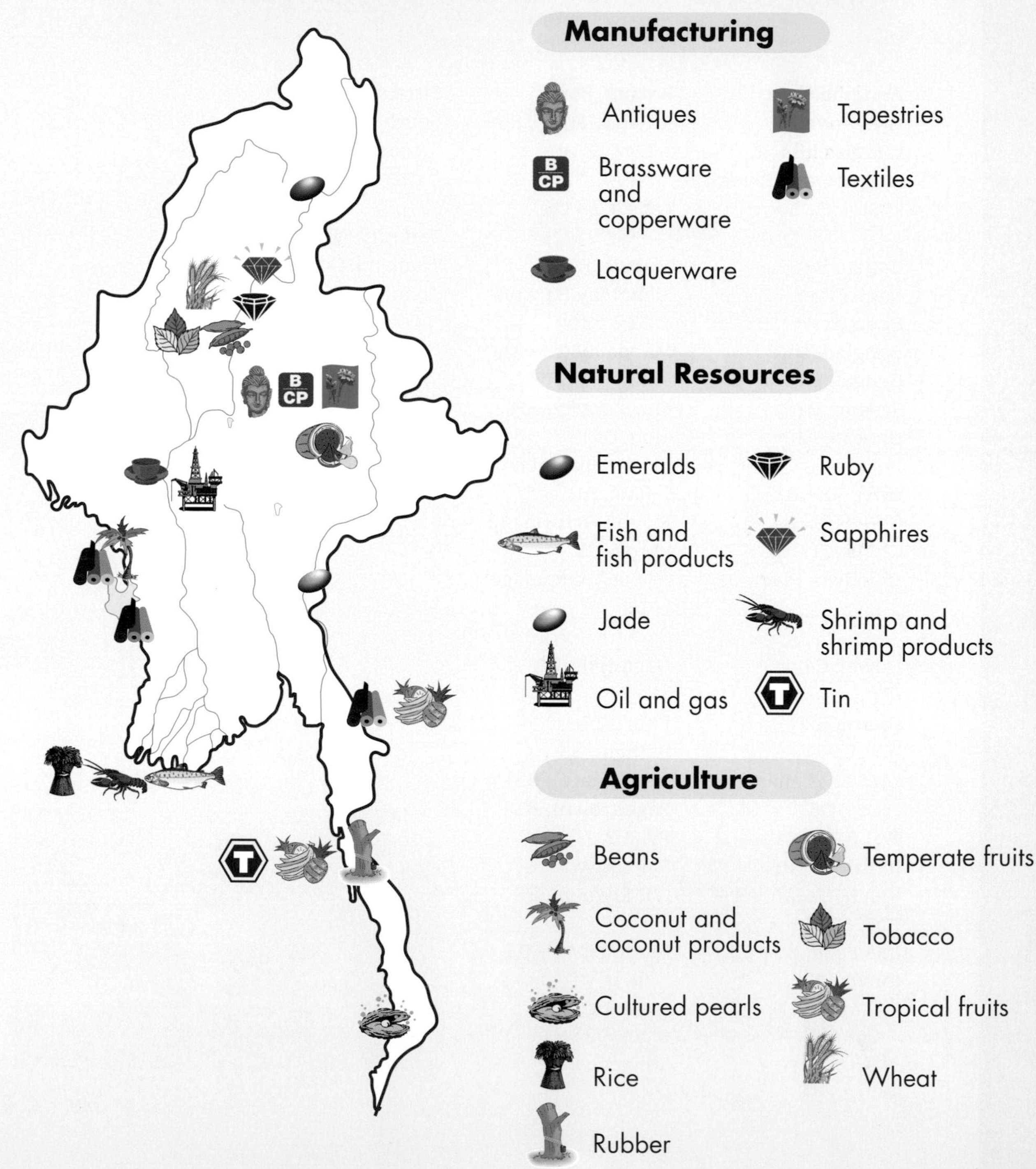

ABOUT THE ECONOMY

OVERVIEW
Myanmar's GDP structure remains the same as it has for decades: agriculture 43.1 percent, industries 19.8 percent, services 37.1 percent.

POPULATION
53.414 million (2010 estimate)

GROSS DOMESTIC PRODUCT
$57.49 billion (2009 estimate)

GDP GROWTH
1.8 percent (2009 estimate)

LAND USE
Arable land: 14.92 percent
Permanent crops: 1.31 percent
Other: 83.77 percent (2005 estimate)

AGRICULTURAL PRODUCTS
Rice, pulses, beans, sesame, groundnuts, sugarcane, hardwood, fish and fish products

MINERAL RESOURCES
Oil and natural gas, jade, gems, copper, tin, tungsten and iron

INFLATION RATE
6.5 percent (2009 estimate)

CURRENCY
US$1=Ks 6.41 (June 2011)
Kyats (Ks) and pyas; 100 pyas=Ks 1.

TOTAL EXPORTS
$6.845 billion (2009 estimate)

MAJOR EXPORTS
Natural gas, teak, beans, pulses, rice, peas, prawns, clothing, jade, and gems

TOTAL IMPORTS
$3.974 billion (2009 estimate)

MAJOR IMPORTS
Fabric, petroleum products, fertilizer, plastics, machinery, transport equipment, cement, construction materials, crude oil, food products, and edible oil

MAIN TRADING PARTNERS
Singapore, Thailand, China, India, Malaysia, and Japan

EXTERNAL DEBT
$7.373 billion (2009 estimate)

WORKFORCE
Age: 15—59 years
Working population: 30.85 million (2009 estimate)

UNEMPLOYMENT RATE
4.9 percent (2009 estimate)

HIGHWAYS
16,777 miles/27,000 km (2006 estimate)

RAILROADS
2,457 miles/3,955 km (2008 estimate)

CULTURAL MYANMAR

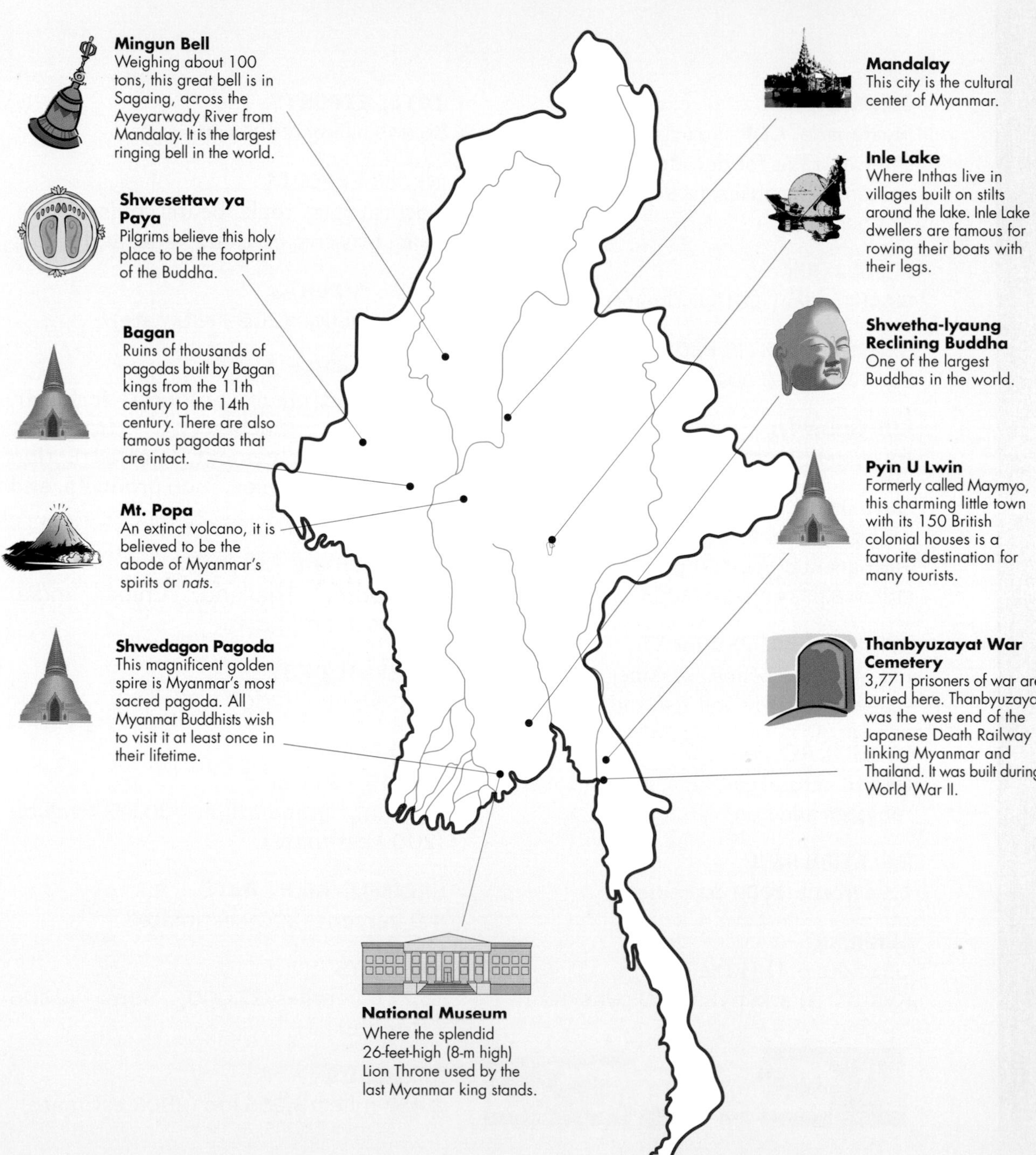

ABOUT THE CULTURE

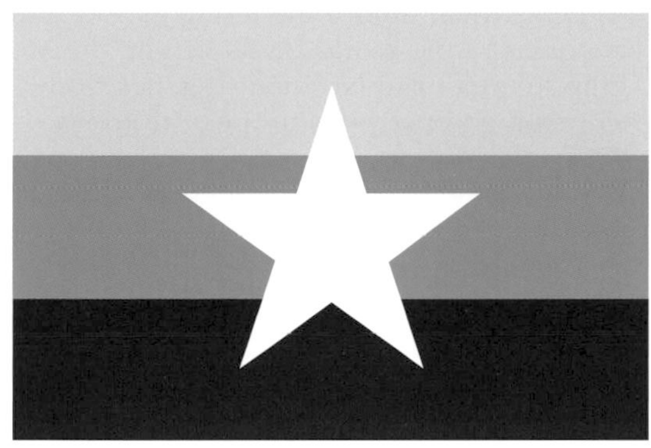

OFFICIAL NAME

Republic of the Union of Myanmar

FLAG DESCRIPTION

On October 21, 2010, the flag was changed to a horizontal tricolor flag of yellow at the top, dark green in the center and red at the bottom, with a single white star in the middle.

LAND AREA

261,228 square miles (67,658 square km)

CAPITAL

Naypyitaw

AGE STRUCTURE

0—14 years: 25.3 percent
(male 6,193,263; female 5,990,658)
15—64 years: 69.3 percent
(male 16,510,648; female 16,828,462)
65 years and over: 5.4 percent
(male 1,121,412; female 1,493,298) (2010 estimate)

POPULATION GROWTH RATE

1.096 percent (2010 estimate)

BIRTHRATE

19.49 births/1,000 population (2010 estimate)

DEATH RATE

8.23 deaths/1,000 population (2010 estimate)

ETHNIC GROUPS

Bamar: 68 percent, Shan: 9 percent, Karen: 7 percent, Rakhine: 4 percent, Chinese: 3 percent, Mon: 2 percent, Indian: 2 percent, other: 5 percent

RELIGIONS

Buddhist: 89 percent, Christian: 4 percent (Baptist: 3 percent, Roman Catholic: 1 percent), Muslim: 4 percent, animist: 1 percent, other: 2 percent

LANGUAGES

Burmese; minority ethnic groups have their own languages

LITERACY

89.9 percent of population age 15 and above (2006 estimate)

IMPORTANT ANNIVERSARIES

Independence Day, January 4; Union Day, February 12; Armed Forces Day, March 7

LEADERS IN POLITICS

General Ne Win: former Chairman of the previous BSPP and President of Myanmar; General Aung San: father of Burma's independence; Daw Aung San Suu Kyi: General Secretary, National League for Democracy

TIME LINE

IN MYANMAR	IN THE WORLD
A.D. 1057 King Anawrahta defeats the Mons and sets up the First Myanmar Empire.	**1206–1368** Genghis Khan unifies the Mongols and starts conquest of the world. At its height, the Mongol Empire under Kublai Khan stretches from China to Persia and parts of Europe and Russia.
	1776 U.S. Declaration of Independence
	1789–99 The French Revolution
1824–26 Burma loses the first Anglo-Myanmar war. Treaty of Yandabo is signed.	
1852 Second Anglo-Myanmar war. The British take control of Lower Myanmar.	
1885–86 Third Anglo-Myanmar war. Myanmar is ruled as a province of British India.	
	1914 World War I begins.
1937 Myanmar is separated from India and becomes a crown colony of Britain.	
	1939 World War II begins.
1942 Japan invades and occupies Myanmar.	
	1945 The United States drops atomic bombs on Hiroshima and Nagasaki. World War II ends.
1948 Myanmar gains independence. U Nu becomes prime minister.	
1962 General Ne Win comes into power following a military coup.	
1974 The Socialist Republic of the Union of Burma is created.	
1989 Aung San Suu Kyi, leader of the National League for Democracy (NLD), is placed under house arrest. She is released in 1995, but is re-arrested in 2000.	
1990 Elections held for the first time in 30 years. NLD wins a landslide victory, but the result is ignored.	

IN MYANMAR	IN THE WORLD
1997 Myanmar joins Association of South East Asian Nations (ASEAN).	**1997** Hong Kong is returned to China.
	2001 Terrorists crash planes into New York, Washington D.C., and Pennsylvania.
2002 Aung San Suu Kyi is released after 20 months of house arrest.	
2003 Aung San Suu Kyi is taken into "protective custody." Khin Nyunt becomes prime minister.	**2003** War in Iraq begins.
	2004 Eleven Asia countries are hit by giant tsunami, killing at least 225,000 people.
	2005 Hurricane Katrina devastates the Gulf Coast of the United States.
2006 Nay Pyi Taw becomes the new capital.	
2007 Military government closes the National Convention, declaring 14 years of constitutional talks complete. Buddhist monks protest against the government.	
2008 Government proposes a new constitution, bans Aung San Suu Kyi from holding office. Cyclone Nargis strikes Ayeyarwady delta, leaving 138,000 people dead or missing. Junta renews Aung San Suu Kyi's house arrest.	**2008** Earthquake in Sichuan, China, kills 67,000 people.
2009 Aung San Suu Kyi is convicted of breaching conditions of her house arrest.	**2009** Outbreak of flu virus H1N1 around the world
2010 Government changes country's flag, national anthem, and official name. General elections held. NLD votes to boycott polls. Myanmar's main military-backed political party, Union Solidarity and Development Party (USDP), reports that it has won about 80 percent of the votes. A week after the election, Aung San Suu Kyi is released from house arrest.	
	2011 Twin earthquake and tsunami disasters strike northeast Japan, leaving over 14,000 dead and thousands more missing.

GLOSSARY

aingyi **(AYN-jee)**
Myanmar blouse or shirt.

biryani
Indian rice dish with chicken and spices.

coup d'état
The violent overthrow of an existing government.

Daw
Honorific for adult female.

Dhamma
Teachings of the Buddha, also spelled "Dharma."

jaggery
Palm sugar balls eaten as a dessert with plain tea.

Jataka
Tales from the Buddha's life.

kadawt **(ker-DORHT)**
Gesture of homage or obeisance.

koon-it **(KOON-it)**
Betel box for putting in the ingredients for chewing betel.

kyat
Monetary unit of Myanmar.

mandat **(MAHN-dat)**
A marquee-like structure made of bamboo matting and bamboo poles.

merit
To better one's life in this and future existences, one has to gain merit through performances of good deeds, such as giving alms to the monks.

mohinga **(mo-HIN-GAH)**
Rice noodles in fish soup, eaten at breakfast.

nat **(nah-t)**
Spirit.

pandan **(PAHN-dan)**
Screw pine plant whose leaves are used for their flavor and to obtain green color in cakes and other desserts.

sadhu **(SAR-doo)**
Pali word meaning "well done," repeated three times after a Buddhist ceremony.

saya
Honorific for teacher or elder.

thanaka **(tha-ner-KAH)**
Pale yellow paste applied to face and arms of women to protext their skin and keep cool.

U
Honorific for a male adult.

zat **(ZAHT)**
Traditional Myanmar drama.

FOR FURTHER INFORMATION

BOOKS

MacLean, Rory. *Under The Dragon: A Journey Through Burma*. London: I B Taurus & Co Ltd. 2008.

Steinberg, David I. *Burma/Myanmar: What Everyone Needs to Know*. New York: Oxford University Press, Inc, 2010.

WEBSITES

Human rights report on Myanmar (1998). www.state.gov/www/global/human_rights/1998_hrp_report/burma.html

Lonely Planet: Myanmar. www.lonelyplanet.com/myanmar-burma

Ministry of Foreign Affairs. www.mofa.gov.mm

Official Website of the Myanmar government. www.myanmar.com

The New Light of Myanmar, a daily newspaper. www.myanmar.com/newspaper/nlm/

DVDS

Raising the Bamboo Curtain: Vietnam, Cambodia and Burma (Myanmar). Rick Ray Films, 1997.

Global Treasures BAGAN Myanmar. TravelVideoStore.com, 2007.

7 Days Myanmar/Burma. TravelVideoStore.com, 2007.

BIBLIOGRAPHY

Houghton, Graham and Wakefield, Julie. *Burma*. London: Macmillan's Children Books, 1988.

Kyi, Aung San Suu. *Burma: Let's Visit Places and Peoples (Illustrated)*. London: Chelsea House, 1988.

Kyi, Aung San Suu. *Freedom From Fear and Other Writings*. London: Penguin Books, 1991.

Kyi, Aung San Suu. *The Voice of Hope: Conversations with Alan Clements*. New York: Seven Stories Press, 1997.

Taik, Aung Aung. *Under the Golden Pagoda: The Best of Burmese Cooking*. San Francisco: Chronicle Books, 1993.

MOVIES (VIDEO)

Beyond Rangoon (1995) starring Patricia Arquette, directed by John Boorman: Plot woven around the 1988 uprising in Myanmar. Filmed in Penang, Malaysia.

INDEX

INDEX